VICTORIAN PHOTOGRAPHY

A somewhat jaundiced view of a daguerreotypist
at work, from Cuthbert Bede's book
Photographic Pleasures, 1855.

PHOTOGRAPHED BY THE PATENT
Van Der Weyde Light
Sole Licensees for
Birmingham

Bernasconi & Co.

20 Colmore Row
Next door to the Birmingham
Dudley & District Bank
Birmingham

PORTRAITS TAKEN FROM 10 A.M. TO 10 P.M.

THE BIRMINGHAM
Photographic
Enlarging
Company,
Studio,
50, New Street,
Offices,
25a, Edgbaston St

COPIES UP TO LIFE SIZE PRINTED IN
SILVER OR PATENT AUTOTYPES & CAN BE
FINISHED IN OIL, CRAYON, OR WATER COLOR.

By Appointment
TO
Her Majesty
John Collier
ROBERT W. THRUPP
66, New Street
BIRMINGHAM
(NEGATIVES KEPT)
COPIES CAN ALWAYS BE OBTAINED

This or any other Portrait
enlarged up to life size and painted in
Oil or Water colors to order.

FROM THE
NEW PHOTOGRAPHIC STUDIO.
Jas Fletcher.
Photographer.
232,
Lichfield Road.
ASTON
Late of 148, Wheeler Street, BIRMINGHAM.

ADDITIONAL COPIES MAY BE HAD AT ANY TIME

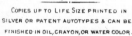

BY SPECIAL APPOINTMENT.
J. T. HADEN
PHOTOGRAPHER
TO
HIS EXCELLENCY THE
LORD LIEUTENANT
OF IRELAND
AND PATRONIZED BY
H.R.H.
THE PRINCE OF WALES
AND H.R.H.
THE DUKE OF CAMBRIDGE

255, Broad Street
BIRMINGHAM
ESTABLISHED 1854.

COPIES OF THIS PORTRAIT CAN BE OBTAINED
AT ANY TIME.
THIS OR ANY OTHER PORTRAIT ENLARGED TO ORDER
& PAINTED IN OIL OR WATER COLOR.

1881

GROUPS
TAKEN BY APPOINTMENT
ANIMALS PHOTOGRAPHED
PICTURE FRAMING
Geo Hynd
PHOTOGRAPHER
King's Heath
ENLARGEMENTS AT MODERATE CHARGES
ALL NEGATIVES PRESERVED
Copies may always be obtained.

N° 24504

BY SPECIAL APPOINTMENT.
PHOTOGRAPHER
TO THE QUEEN.

H. J. WHITLOCK.
11. NEW STREET,
BIRMINGHAM.

THE ORIGINAL NEGATIVE OF THIS PORTRAIT
IS RETAINED AND COPIES CAN BE SUPPLIED.

N° 11631

H. J. WHITLOCK

PHOTOGRAPHED BY
H. J. Whitlock
11, NEW STREET
BIRMINGHAM

NEGATIVES KEPT AND ORDERS
FOR PRINTS PROMPTLY EXECUTED

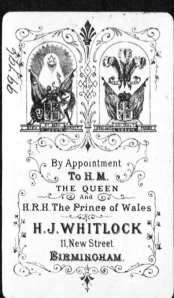

By Appointment
To H.M.
THE QUEEN
And
H.R.H. The Prince of Wales
H.J. WHITLOCK
11, New Street
BIRMINGHAM.

VICTORIAN PHOTOGRAPHY

An Introduction for Collectors and Connoisseurs

B.E.C. HOWARTH-LOOMES

St. Martin's Press
New York

ERRATA
Captions to colour illustrations should read:

Page 17   *Left: Seven stereoscopes in wood,* papier-mâché, *tortoiseshell and leather. A large number of viewers sold were designed as attractive pieces for the drawingroom, rather than as efficient optical viewers.*

Page 33   *Left: Nine carte-de-visite albums. Highly decorated or unusual albums are themselves the subject of collection; generally dating from about 1870 onwards their contents are often of little photographic interest.*

To the Antique Dealers and 'Junk Boys'
whose patience, tolerance and kindness
I have so frequently strained.

Frontispiece

The backs of cartes by Birmingham photographers.
Despite much learned research into the history of photography,
there is little detailed information available regarding
cartes-de-visite. A collector specializing in cartes originating
from his own area, has the opportunity of compiling an
authorative index of local photographers and their dates from
sources such as borough archives. There is a great variety of
design on the back; even the same photographer varies over the
years, but in general, the simpler the design, the earlier the
carte is likely to be.

ACKNOWLEDGEMENTS

The author is indebted to the staffs of various museums and
libraries throughout the country for their kind assistance and
trusts they will accept a general acknowledgement dictated
by lack of space. He wishes to thank the following in
particular for help beyond the normal call of duty or
friendship: Miss Alma Blyde; Mrs Helga Castle; Mr Peter
Castle, Victoria & Albert Museum, London; Mr Brian Coe,
Kodak Museum; Mr A. M. H. Rumsey; Dr David Thomas,
Science Museum.

The author and publishers would like to thank the following
for permission to reproduce illustrations: Aberdeen Public
Library 96/3; Dr Barnardo's 85/1, 2; Bayerisches
Nationalmuseum, Munich 19/3; E. A. Blyde 19/2; The
Bodleian Library 29/2, 45/3, 74/5, 77/1, 2, 99/1; British
Museum 44/2; Miss Elizabeth Clifford 67/1; Edinburgh
Public Libraries 26/4, 38, 42, 43, 45/4, 46/4, 92, 99/4; Mr
David Francis 58/2, 74/6, 89/4, 91/1, 95/1; The International
Museum of Photography, New York 28/4, 36/1, 37/3, 56/4;
Kenneth and Jenny Jacobson 64/2; The Kodak Museum 6,
13/2, 3, 15, 16/1, 2, 4, 5, 18/2, 27/1, 29/1, 34/2, 35/1, 2, 36/3,
37/1, 44/3, 45/1, 2, 47/1, 49/1, 50, 52/2, 56/2, 3, 57/2, 65,
66-7, 67/2, 74/4, 75/5, 77/4, 79/7, 85/3, 4, 86/1, 94/1, 2, 96/4,
98/1; London Transport 54; Mr Peter MacTaggart 86/3;
Museum of the History of Science, Oxford 44/1, 52/1;
National Army Museum 41; National Galleries of Scotland
27/3, 47/2, 48/1; National Monuments Records 40, 59/3, 63,
97/3; Pilkington Glass Co. Ltd 87/1, 2, 89/2; Royal College
of Surgeons 20, 53/2, 77/3, 90/4; Royal Microscopical
Society 25/3; Royal Scottish Museum 25/2, 6; J. Sainsbury
Ltd 96/2; Mr David Scheinmann 64/1; Science Museum 10,
12, 13/1, 14/5, 16/3, 17, 18/1, 19/1, 22-3, 46/3, 73/1, 74/2,
75/2, 78/4, 5, 7, 97/2; Southampton City Museums 87/3;
M. M. Stallick 37/2; Victoria & Albert Museum 9/1, 31/1,
33/4, 44/4, 46/1, 2, 60/1, 62, 94-5; The Webb Collection
28/1, 30/3, 32/1, 3, 4, 33/3, 34/3, 36/2, 4, 53/2, 73/2; The
Wills Collection 2, 9/2, 28/3, 99/2.

Contents

All prices are at the rate of $4.00 to £1·00 – the Victorian exchange-rate.

Introduction

In the spring of 1972, a major exhibition of Victorian photography was mounted at the Victoria and Albert Museum in London. Since then, auctions of Victorian photographs and photographic equipment in the London sale rooms have become a regular occurrence. Television and magazines have devoted time and space to the subject and a week seldom passes without some mention of nineteenth century photography appearing in the national press. A spate of books is available on Victorian photographers or Victorian photography, and old photographs are used in yet more books to illustrate some point or other. Antique shops now proudly display photographic items that once would have been left to grace the totter's barrow – or even thrown into the dealer's dust bin as rubbish. Several antique dealers specialize in nineteenth century photographic apparatus. Victorian photography has become an 'in' subject. Fashion has caught up with that faded sepia-toned image of Great-Grandmother.

With record prices being announced for old cameras, and single photographic prints by some well-known Victorian photographers fetching prices well into three figures – and sometimes nearer four – it may be thought that early photography is yet another subject from which the collector with limited means is excluded. Fortunately, however, this is far from being so. If the would-be collector has dreams of forming a collection of daguerreotype cameras or original prints by Fox Talbot, the chances are that he will be disappointed unless Lady Luck shows him more favour than she has shown to many collectors of considerable experience. If his sights are set at a slightly lower level, there is little to prevent him building a collection that will provide a great deal of pleasure.

For anyone not previously interested in early photography, it would be excusable to think that, until recently, Victorian photography was completely unknown and that information regarding its discovery, development and use had only just been announced. Such a belief would be understandable but very mistaken.

The major London museums have been actively collecting material since the early 1850s and many other museums had built up collections by the end of the last century. A Keeper of Film and Photography has recently been appointed in the National Portrait Gallery to attend to its collection. In many other countries, including America, France and Germany, there has been an awareness of the historical importance of early photography for many years. Learned and private societies also hold valuable collections. The Royal Photographic Society has been accepting gifts since its inception in 1853.

In the commercial sector, many companies have kept photographs that relate to their beginnings and, although few go back to the earliest days of photography, they form a useful source of historical material. Kodak Ltd established a museum in 1927 which now ranks among the major photographic museums in Britain.

Individuals have been active for many years, and several excellent private collections exist, ranging from those which demonstrate the wide range of photographic history to collections based on specific areas such as various types of cameras or photographs. Some collectors have chosen books illustrated by photographs, or books and pamphlets about photography. Then there are the subjects that are not basically photographic but which involve some photography, such as magic lanterns, which predate the invention of photography but later used photographic slides. The fact that photographs are collected by people who are interested, not in photography but in subjects as widely diverse as early advertising or the history of the Boer War, is an indication of the very wide impact that photography has had on society.

Few would-be collectors sit down and think about what to collect. Generally something catches their eye and is bought on impulse. Later another pleasing item is seen and the fact that it relates in some way to a previous purchase justifies further expenditure. This can happen eight or nine times before the person is aware that he has become a collector. It is at this point that the new collector should consider his position. Two choices are available. He, or she, for collecting is by no means a male prerogative, can try and assemble a collection that will show the broad development of photography from its beginnings to the present day. The second choice is to limit the collection to a specific

Left: *A calotype by H. V. Regnault of the entrance to the porcelain factory at Sevres. Regnault, a leading French physicist, was an enthusiastic amateur photographer and a founder member of the first photographic society,* the Société Heliographique, *formed in Paris in January 1851.*

area of the subject. There are advantages and disadvantages to either choice.

Photography in the nineteenth century covered such a wide field that, in any antique or junk market, there will be something for sale that has some part in the history of photography. No matter how assiduously the markets are combed, the collection will never be complete. After years of collecting and increasing knowledge, there will be items, perhaps worth only pennies, that are still wanted. This type of general collecting also requires considerable storage space.

The problems arising from the second choice depend on the area chosen. Storage space may again have to be considered. Cameras, photographic albums and stereoscopes take up a large amount of room. Even photographs can present a storage problem when the collection has grown to several thousand photographic prints. A main disadvantage of limiting the collection to a specific area is that, eventually, it may become increasingly difficult to find fresh items, not already in the collection, at a moderate cost.

Where and what to buy can only be learned through experience. It may encourage the new collector to find that he is not alone in making mistakes. The descriptions of items that appear in some of the sale catalogues leave much to be desired in the way of accuracy, and some are positively funny. There are, however, some steps that can be taken to avoid a few of the more obvious mistakes. If possible, visit museums that possess collections in the field in which you are interested. Some of the collections on public display are listed in this book. There are also several books in print dealing with various aspects of photographic history that repay reading. A selection of such books is

Above right: A calotype by Blanquart-Evrard of the Porte Rouge, Paris, c. 1847.

Below: The periods of most common occurrence of the principle forms of photographs are indicated on this chart.

also given. Museum curators are invariably helpful and tend to be more so when it is obvious that the collector has first tried to find the information he is seeking for himself. Fellow collectors are another source of information. Attend sales, but remember that it may be cheaper for prosperous collectors, to whom time is money, to compete with each other at auctions rather than spend days hunting around to find well-stocked antique shops.

It is difficult, if not impossible, to give advice on values. Generally speaking, the prices realised in the main London auction rooms are at the very top end of the scale and there is a marked tendency for prices to rise, although there have been one or two instances of them falling.

It is from antique shops that the bulk of the collection will come. Antique dealers are an odd race, and no general advice can be offered for dealing with such a peculiar section of the population. The vast majority of dealers are surprisingly helpful and reasonable in their prices, although any man who willingly adopts an occupation in which many of his customers will be collectors of one sort or another, must be slightly mad.

This book does not set out to advise on what to collect, or how to collect. Neither is it a history of the subject. Its purpose is to entertain and introduce some of the fascinating photography of that remarkable breed of men and women, the Victorians.

One sombre note of warning must be given. Collecting is an addictive disease. A glazed look in the listener's eye as the collector talks about his hobby is the first symptom. The author, whose family have suffered from his symptoms for many years, is of the opinion that the disease is irreversible.

Below right: With the introduction of Scott Archer's patent-free process, many books and pamphlets became available for both the amateur and professional. Such books complete with their advertisements, are an important source of information.

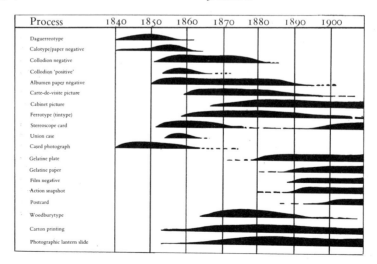

Process	1840	1850	1860	1870	1880	1890	1900
Daguerreotype							
Calotype/paper negative							
Collodion negative							
Collodion 'positive'							
Albumen paper negative							
Carte-de-visite picture							
Cabinet picture							
Ferrotype (tintype)							
Stereoscope card							
Union case							
Cased photograph							
Gelatine plate							
Gelatine paper							
Film negative							
Action snapshot							
Postcard							
Woodburytype							
Carton printing							
Photographic lantern slide							

1 The Invention of Photography

In the first month of 1839, two photographic processes were announced to the civilized world and, within ten years, several million photographs had been produced.

It is impossible to say when the very first steps were taken that led eventually to the discovery of photography. To produce a photograph, a camera and a surface sensitive to light are required. After exposing the sensitized surface in the camera, the image must in some way be fixed before the continued effect of the light causes the image to vanish. An understanding of chemistry and a knowledge of optics had to be brought together before the first practical experiments could take place.

The optics required presented little difficulty to the early experimentalists. It had been known for centuries that if, during the hours of daylight, a small hole was made in the wall of a darkened room, an image would be projected on the wall opposite the hole. Such rooms were in use in the fifteenth century and enabled the early scientists to study the eclipse of the sun. Even then it was not a new discovery. The Arabian scholar, Alhazen, had described the principles involved in the eleventh century, and in the fourth century BC the Chinese had observed and recorded the phenomenon.

Throughout the years, improvements were made to the *camera obscura* (from the latin meaning a dark room) and a variety of types were made, including portable devices in which the observer sat. Gradually its main use became that of an aid to artists and, by the end of the eighteenth century, a small model, employing a lens and reflecting mirror, was in fairly widespread use. It was this instrument that was to be used in the first practical experiments leading to the invention of photography.

Man's first knowledge of chemistry and the effects of light on certain substances must have begun very early indeed. Primitive man would have noticed that his dyes lasted longer in the cave than they did exposed to the sunlight, and thousands of years later, alchemists searching for gold knew some of the reactions caused by light.

Early in the seventeenth century, when alchemy had given way to chemistry, Angelo Sala noted that powdered silver nitrate would blacken if exposed to sunlight. He published his observations in a pamphlet in Amsterdam in 1614, but it was more than a hundred years later that this property of silver nitrate was employed to make an image. Johann Heinrich Schulze, a professor in Bavaria, experimented with silver nitrate in 1725. He covered a jar containing the chemical with a paper stencil and placed it in sunlight. When the stencil was removed, those parts that had remained covered were unaffected, but the areas that had been exposed to light had darkened.

About 1800, optics and chemistry came together in the hands of Thomas Wedgwood of the pottery family. He attempted to produce a picture by exposing a suitable surface coated with silver nitrate in a *camera obscura,* but the results were unsatisfactory. Using paper coated with silver nitrate, he then tried placing a variety of objects, including ferns, leaves and paintings on glass, on top of the paper and exposing to light. The result was a clear image with the light and shaded areas of the original object being reversed on the image. Other materials that he experimented with included light-coloured leather and he noticed that the silver nitrate responded much more quickly to light on the leather than it had on the paper. It was found that the tannin contained gallic acid, an ingredient that later was to be widely used in photography. However, despite many experiments, Wedgwood was unable to fix the images he had produced and, when exposed to light, they soon faded.

Many writers on photography have commented on a curious fact. The Wedgwood family had, among their friends, many of the leading scientists of the day, including Sir Humphry Davy who was known to be aware of the experiments of a Swedish chemist named Scheel. These experiments had shown that if silver chloride is exposed to light, it is reduced to a black deposit of metallic silver and any unexposed silver chloride present can be dissolved by ammonia. Apparently Davy did not think of applying this knowledge to Wedgwood's process by using ammonia to dissolve the unexposed silver nitrate and thus fix his images. A few years later, Wedgwood died aged 34, having come very close to inventing photography.

The effects of the continuing industrial revolution were producing changes in social patterns. New cities

Left: A positive print from Talbot's paper negative (much enlarged).

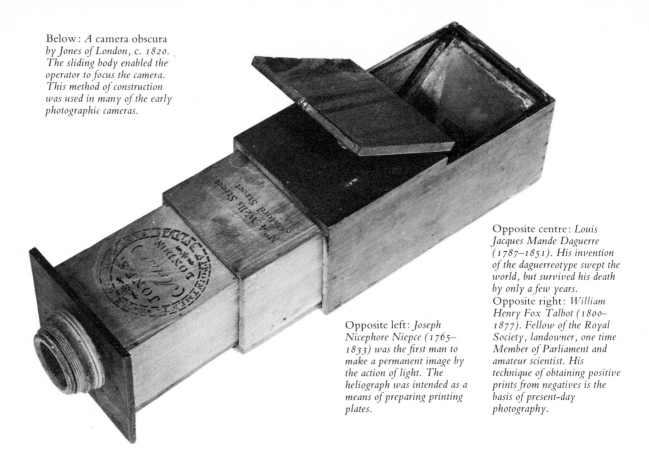

Below: *A camera obscura by Jones of London, c. 1820. The sliding body enabled the operator to focus the camera. This method of construction was used in many of the early photographic cameras.*

Opposite left: *Joseph Nicephore Niepce (1765–1833) was the first man to make a permanent image by the action of light. The heliograph was intended as a means of preparing printing plates.*

Opposite centre: *Louis Jacques Mande Daguerre (1787–1851). His invention of the daguerreotype swept the world, but survived his death by only a few years.*
Opposite right: *William Henry Fox Talbot (1800–1877). Fellow of the Royal Society, landowner, one time Member of Parliament and amateur scientist. His technique of obtaining positive prints from negatives is the basis of present-day photography.*

were being created and existing cities enlarged. The birth rate was increasing and there was a general movement of population towards the main industrial centres. A relatively new social class began to emerge; managers, professional groups, business men and others of similar income and backgrounds gradually formed what became known as the middle class. It was a class that demanded – and received – things that, before its appearance, would have been available only to the very wealthy. It was a class fully aware of its position, and it wanted the services to which it felt it was entitled and able to afford. The majority of the English public schools were built in the nineteenth century to educate its sons. The large number of charities that were established demonstrated its social awareness. Portraits, once available to the very wealthy only, could be commissioned by a far wider range of people. Silhouettes and physionotraces, which possessed the merit of being cheaper, were popular. Books illustrated by engravings were in demand and slowly the emphasis moved from quality to quantity. At the end of the eighteenth century, lithography was invented. In very simple terms, a lithograph is made by drawing the design required on a smooth flat stone with a greasy crayon. The stone is moistened and ink applied to the surface, the ink holding only to the

crayon. Paper is then pressed to the surface to make a print. This method of obtaining prints needed less skill and was cheaper than the engraving process. It became very popular in many countries, including France.

Joseph Nicéphore Niépce was a retired French army officer living near Chalon in eastern France. He knew, and had used, the *camera obscura* for many years and when lithography became known, he greeted the new process with enthusiasm. Two difficulties faced him. No stone suitable for the lithographic plates was available locally and Niépce was unable to draw. The first problem was overcome by using pewter for the plates and the second was resolved by Niépce looking after the chemical and printing side of the work whilst his son attended to the drawing. It was an arrangement that worked well until the son, Isidore, joined the army and Joseph began to look for another method of obtaining drawings for his plates.

Niépce knew of the sensitivity to light of various chemicals and began his experiments by obtaining prints, as Wedgwood had done, by placing transparent engravings on sensitized surfaces. Later he turned to the *camera obscura* and tried to capture and hold the image the camera produced. Pewter plates, coated with a type of bitumen, were exposed in the camera for long periods and then washed in a mixture

of oil of lavender and white petroleum. The bitumen used by Niépce possessed the characteristic of becoming insoluble when exposed to light so that, when the plate was washed in the solution, the unexposed parts of the bitumen were dissolved, leaving the image fixed permanently on the plate. The earliest surviving example, showing a view from a window of Niépce's home, is generally believed to have been taken about 1827.

In the same year, Niépce came into contact with Louis Jacques Mandé Daguerre and, three years later, a partnership agreement was signed by the two men covering their joint work to improve the process. When Niépce died in 1833 his son Isidore succeeded his father as Daguerre's partner.

Daguerre was a very different man from Niépce. Although he claimed to be working on the same lines as Niépce, he had not succeeded in producing a permanent image at the time the agreement was signed. By profession he was a painter and showman, best known for his Diorama presentations, one of which was opened near Regents Park in London in 1823. He was one of the few pioneers of photography to have had little or no scientific training or experience. He continued the experiments and, by 1835, had made such progress that Isidore was persuaded to accept an alteration in the partnership agreement that was in Daguerre's favour. By 1837, Daguerre had produced a clear permanent picture showing a corner of his studio. This plate was presented to the curator of the Louvre and is now in the possession of the French Photographic Society in Paris.

The process developed by Daguerre involved taking a copper plate that had been silver-plated and coating it with silver iodide. The plate was then placed in the camera and exposed for a period of up to an hour. Having been removed from the camera, the plate was then placed over a dish of heated mercury. When the image had appeared, the plate was then washed in a solution of salt in distilled water. After drying the plate, the picture was ready to be shown. The image produced was a positive and it was impossible to make further prints from the plate.

On 7 January 1839, an announcement was made in Paris that M. Daguerre had succeeded in taking pictures from nature. The public announcement of the new invention caused great excitement but, in a small village in Wiltshire, one man received the news with dismay.

In October of the same year in which Joseph Niépce died, William Henry Fox Talbot, an upper-class English gentleman of Lacock Abbey in Wiltshire, was sketching on the bank of Lake Como using a *camera lucida* as an aid to his drawing. Dissatisfied with the results of his sketching, he recalled the clear images projected onto paper by the *camera obscura* and decided that, on his return to England, he would begin experiments in an attempt 'to cause these natural images to imprint themselves durably and remain fixed upon the paper'. At this time, Fox Talbot did not know of the experiments made by Wedgwood and Niépce. After returning to England in the early part of 1834, Talbot began his experiments. His first results were obtained by placing leaves and cuttings of lace on sensitized paper. Although this method gave an image, the reaction to light of the silver nitrate with which the paper was coated was too slow. He discovered that if he first impregnated the paper with a mild solution of salt before coating with silver nitrate, the exposure time was improved. Too strong a solution of salt, however, produced the reverse effect. He used this knowledge to fix the image after exposure by washing the exposed paper in a strong solution of salt. The resulting image he called Photogenic Drawings.

Talbot's first attempts to procure a picture by using sensitized paper in the *camera obscura* were not satisfactory. After an exposure of more than an hour, he found the images to be faint and showing no detail. He reasoned that if he employed a smaller camera, the image would be imprinted on the paper in a shorter time. Several small cameras were made by the local carpenter and Talbot fitted each with a lens having a

Above: *The earliest extant photograph on glass. It shows scaffolding around a telescope and was taken by Herschel in September 1839.*

Left: *A heliotype from a plate prepared by Niepce in 1826.*

Right: *The earliest surviving image. Taken by Niepce from a window of his home in 1827, it required an exposure of eight hours. Due to the difficulty of photographing the faint image of the original, defects in the surface of the plate are somewhat emphasized.*

focal length of about two inches. Using one of these cameras, Talbot produced a clear picture of one of the windows of Lacock Abbey in 1835. However, where the light had affected the paper, the image was darkened, resulting in the shades being reversed. What Talbot had produced was the world's first negative. Although the image was only about an inch square, Talbot was able to count the 200 panes of glass by using a lens to magnify the picture.

There is some evidence to indicate that Talbot did not attach too much importance to his photogenic drawing experiments, and he complained that he had too little time to experiment. When it is realised that, between 1834 and 1839, he published eleven scientific papers on subjects ranging from the nature of light to a paper on integral calculus, his lack of leisure is hardly surprising. Had Talbot not heard of the work of Daguerre, it is possible that he might have left further experiments for some years. At a meeting of the Royal Institution on 25 January 1839, Michael Faraday announced Talbot's process and examples of Photogenic Drawings were displayed. A few days later, Talbot himself read a paper describing his work to the Institution.

Although a knowledge of the discoveries that resulted in the invention of photography is of help and interest to the collector, his chances of finding any items of this period at a reasonable cost are remote.

Above left: *One of the cameras made to Fox Talbot's order by a local carpenter c. 1835. Mrs. Talbot referred to them as mousetraps.*
Above: *An illustration showing the principle and basic design of an early camera obscura.*
Left: *The earliest surviving negative showing a window at Lacock Abbey, (original size) taken by Fox Talbot in 1835. Although Talbot mentioned that the image had faded, the enlargement clearly shows the details.*

Right: *A whole-plate daguerreotype camera of 1839. Made by Alphonse Giroux of Paris, to whom Daguerre had granted a licence to manufacture and sell cameras, each model carried a seal signed by Daguerre.*

Below: Camera Lucida. *This instrument, although called a camera, is not part of the development of photography. Invented by William Wollaston in 1807 as an aid to sketching, it is sometimes mistakenly thought by inexperienced collectors to be a forerunner of the modern camera.*

Left: *A camera obscura of the type used by Fox Talbot. A number of firms made similar models and although rare, examples do occasionally appear on the market.*

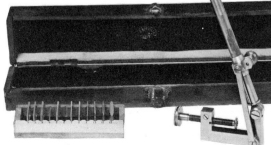

Right: *A selection of typical photographic jewellery. The top eight items contain daguerreotypes; the examples of ambrotypes, tintypes and paper prints also illustrated are common, although unusual mountings are of interest.*

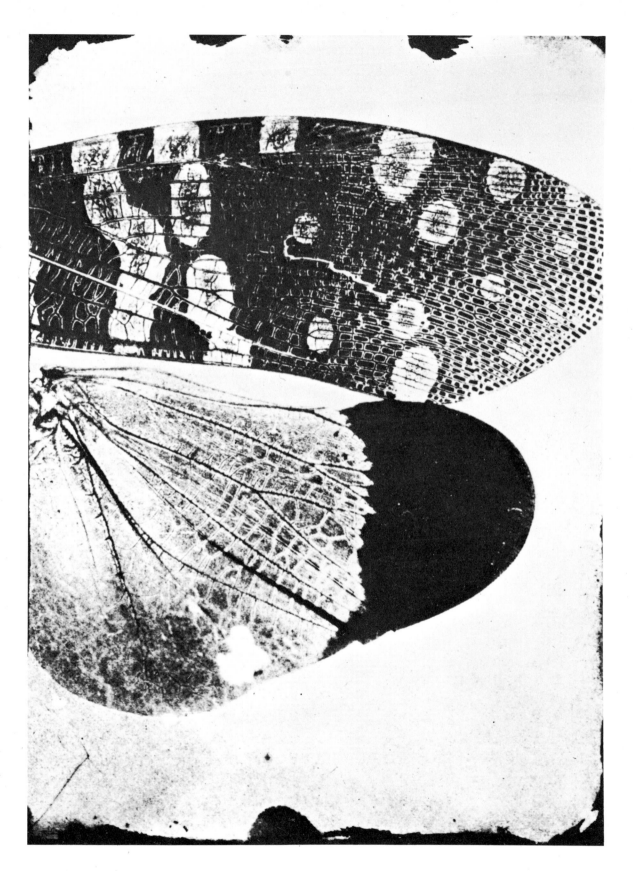

Left: *Nine carte-de-visite albums. Highly decorated or unusual albums are themselves the subject of collection; generally dating from about 1870 onwards their contents are often of little photographic interest.*

Above: *A photomicrograph of insects' wings by Fox Talbot, c. 1839.*

Below: *A photogenic drawing by Fox Talbot. It is not unusual to find examples of this process, but it would be a mistake to assume they belong to the very early period of photography. It was a popular method of getting an image and was used until well into this century. All that was needed was a sheet of sensitized paper, some leaves and a fixing solution.*

Below right: *An engraving showing the making of a silhouette.*

Right: *Title page from the third edition of J. S. Memes' translation of Daguerre's manual, 1839. More than thirty editions of the manual were published during 1839.*

HISTORY AND PRACTICE

OF

PHOTOGENIC DRAWIN

ON THE TRUE PRINCIPLES OF THE

DAGUERRÉOTYPE,

WITH THE NEW METHOD OF

DIORAMIC PAINTING;

SECRETS PURCHASED BY THE FRENCH GOVERNMENT, AND BY THE
COMMAND PUBLISHED FOR THE BENEFIT OF
THE ARTS AND MANUFACTURES:

BY THE INVENTOR

L. J. M. DAGUERRE,

OFFICER OF THE LEGION OF HONOUR, AND MEMBER OF VARIOUS ACADEMI

TRANSLATED FROM THE ORIGINAL BY

J. S. MEMES, LL.D.

HON. MEM. OF THE ROYAL SCOTTISH ACADEMY OF FINE ARTS, ETC.

" As a recompense for giving the secret of this splendid discovery to the world,
French Government has just awarded an Annual Pension of Ten Thousand Francs"

THIRD EDITION.

LONDON:
SMITH, ELDER AND CO., CORNHILL
AND ADAM BLACK AND CO., EDINBURGH.
1839.

Right: *Boulevard du Temple, Paris. Although millions of daguerreotypes were taken, very few by Daguerre himself are known. This street scene taken by Daguerre in 1839 shows the first man to be photographed. Exposure times were too long to permit portraiture but the man having his shoes cleaned remained still long enough for his blurred image to register.*

Below: *Pencil drawing by Sir John Herschel, 1792–1871, sketched by means of a camera lucida in 1824. Herschel was closely involved in the early development of photography and made several important contributions.*

Right: *A charcoal drawing of Margaret McGlusky about 1832. Local or itinerant artists would produce these somewhat stylized portraits for a few shillings. The invention of photography caused considerable hardship among such artists, many of whom turned to colouring photographs, or even became photographers themselves.*

2 The Daguerreotype

Although an announcement concerning Daguerre's work had been made in January, it was not until August 1839 that details were given to the public. On 14 August, Daguerre secured his invention in England by patent and five days later in Paris, the French Government revealed the full process and gave it free to the rest of the world. This, not surprisingly, was to cause considerable ill-feeling towards Daguerre in England.

The new invention was greeted enthusiastically. To people accustomed to looking at paintings and engravings, the clarity and accuracy of the daguerreotype was something at which they marvelled. Public exhibitions were arranged at which Daguerre demonstrated his process before excited audiences. He also prepared a manual and, within a year, more than thirty editions had been printed and sold. Few inventions have received the wide acclaim that was bestowed on the daguerreotype.

It was soon noticed that the process had several defects limiting its commercial possibilities. The exposure required to produce an image was too long to permit portrait photography. Even in the brightest sunlight, the time needed was seldom less than ten minutes. Another disadvantage was the extreme delicacy of the surface. The slightest touch was sufficient to damage the image.

Until 1839, only a few men had been involved in the experiments that led to Daguerre's invention but within months of the publication of the manual, men all over the world examined the process and sought ways to improve it. In Vienna an optician, Joseph Petzval, designed a lens that gave an image sixteen times stronger than the simple lens used by Daguerre. In England, John Goddard suggested exposing the plate to a bromine vapour in addition to iodine to increase the sensitivity to light. These two improvements made portraiture possible. The nature of the surface was strengthened by a discovery of Hippolyte Fizeau. After exposure and fixing, the plate was treated with a heated solution of gold chloride, which also improved the tone of the image.

In 1841, it was possible to take a Daguerreotype in 20 seconds and, by the following year, this time had been halved. Later, depending on the light available and the size of the plate being exposed, it became possible to achieve results in less than a second. Studios opened throughout the world to a public eager to have its likeness recorded on the silvered plate.

America received the Daguerreotype with rapturous delight and, within a few years, most American towns had at least one 'Daguerreian Gallery'. Outlying communities were served by travelling Daguerreotypists, some of whom used wagons fitted out as mobile studios. It has been estimated that, in 1853, there were more than ninety studios in New York alone, and that at least 10,000 people were engaged throughout America in the production of daguerreotypes. John Whipple of Boston employed his American ingenuity to reduce the time spent in preparations by inventing a machine to buff and polish the plates, work previously done by hand. Alexander Wolcott, in collaboration with John Johnson, produced a camera in which the lens was replaced by a concave mirror. The skill of the American Daguerreotypist was demonstrated in 1851 when, at the Crystal Palace Exhibition in London, three of the five medals awarded for daguerreotypes went to Americans.

In France, as may have been expected, the commercial exploitation of the process was immense. N. P. Lerebours was probably the first to open a studio in Paris and, in 1841, is reported to have taken over fifteen hundred portraits. In 1847 alone, more than two thousand cameras and half a million plates were sold in Paris.

The daguerreotype was not limited to portraiture in the towns and cities of Europe and America. Travellers carried cameras to every part of the world and daguerreotypes of landscapes and architectural subjects from such places as China, Australia, Mexico, India and Egypt were exhibited and sold.

In England, the use of the daguerreotype was limited by the effects of Daguerre's patent. Only by purchasing a licence was it permissible to begin operating as a daguerreotypist. Richard Beard, a former coal merchant, opened the first studio in England at the Royal Polytechnic institution in London on 23 March 1841, and so popular was the daguerreotype that, within

Left: *A velvet-lined wooden case, measuring 2' × 2', containing twenty daguerreotype portraits by Jabez Hogg of some of the leading scientists and surgeons of the day. Jabez Hogg, an eminent ophthalmic surgeon, was keenly interested in photography. His* Practical Manual of Photography, *first published in 1843, ran to five editions, and copies can still be found at reasonable prices. Display cases holding collections such as this are very rare and are seldom to be found outside of museums or institutions.*

Panorama of Paris. This daguerreotype was once owned by Fox Talbot.

eighteen months, he had opened seven other studios.

The second man to establish a studio in England was Antoine François Jean Claudet, a Frenchman who had settled in London in 1827. His studio, at the Adelaide Galleries in King William Street, opened in June 1841. Although the quality of much of Claudet's work is excellent, it is perhaps for his many technical contributions to early photography that he is mainly remembered. One of his innovations was the use of background scenery which improved the composition of the image and enabled the operator to have both sitter and background in focus. He was also a pioneer in the colouring of daguerreotypes.

During the following years, many other studios opened throughout Britain and among the best-known are those of T. R. Williams, Edwin Mayall, J. Whitlock and W. E. Kilburn. The majority of daguerreotypes found bear no photographer's name and positive identification of photographer or sitter is usually impossible.

Generally daguerreotypes are fairly small, whole-plate ($6\frac{1}{2}'' \times 8\frac{1}{2}''$) being the unit by which smaller sizes were measured. The cost of having a daguerreotype taken varied according to the dimension and quality of the silvered plate. The most popular sizes were one-eighth plate ($2\frac{1}{8}'' \times 3\frac{1}{4}''$) and one-sixth plate ($2\frac{3}{4}'' \times 3\frac{1}{4}''$). Daguerreotypes of whole-plate size and above are uncommon. The largest-known example measures $29'' \times 25''$ and is in the Science Museum in London.

The method of presenting the daguerreotype was important. Despite the gold toning process, the surface remained delicate and if exposed to the air, tarnishing of the silver would soon obscure the image. The plate was protected by glass and sealed with a paper binding. Frequently a gilt mount was placed between plate and glass, serving to enhance the overall appearance and preventing the glass from coming into contact with the image. The daguerreotype could then be placed in a frame, usually *papier mâché*, suitable for hanging on a wall, or bound in a narrow gilt frame and fitted into a case.

The variety of cases available was considerable. The most common were of wood covered with dark red leather, the inside of the lid being lined with red plush. Some cases have a decorative pattern worked into the leather whilst others bear the photographer's name in gilt. Tortoise shell, decorated *papier mâché*, silver and mother-of-pearl were also used.

From America, very large numbers of 'Union cases' were imported. Shellac and various fillers provided a material that could be moulded into elaborate shapes

and designs when hot and cooled to a hard, but brittle, finish. These cases represent one of the earliest commercial uses of thermoplastic and were first patented in America by Samuel Peck in 1854. The designs employed include geometric patterns, scenes from modern or classical history and portraits of well-known people. Union cases have been a subject for collecting in their own right for some years and examples of the more unusual designs or sizes are now tending to become rare.

The inexperienced collector should remember that cases are not unique to the daguerreotype. They continued in production until after the need for a protective cover for an image had passed.

Although the daguerreotype became immensely popular, it failed to provide a cheap and simple method of reproduction as Niépce had originally intended when he began his experiments. If more than one image was required, either the subject or the daguerreotype had to be re-photographed. Several attempts were made to find a satisfactory system by which the daguerreotype could be used as a printing plate, but none were commercially feasible.

Some engravings and lithographs were produced by the artist copying daguerreotypes and, although this resulted in more accurate prints, there was no saving in cost or time. Examples can be found in most print shops for a few pence. One of the best-known series of engravings, for which the daguerreotype was used as a guide, was *Excursions Daguerriennes,* published between 1840 and 1844 by N. P. Lerebours in Paris. Examples from this series are rare.

Another disadvantage of the daguerreotype was the high degree of reflection from the silvered plate, which meant that the image could be viewed only from certain angles. It is this characteristic that makes daguerreotypes the most easily recognizable of all photographic processes.

The young collector, new to the subject, will make mistakes. A surge of enthusiasm coupled with a lack of experience may lead to an expensive but poor collection. Ask an established collector about his mistakes and a long sad tale will follow. However, ask the same collector about interesting items he missed through inexperience or caution and the embarrassing sight of a grown man reduced to tears may well result.

It is difficult, if not impossible, to offer general advice on the prices that should be paid for any photographic item. Until 1971, it was possible to buy fine daguerreotypes for a few shillings. Such has been the sudden interest in the subject that now a few pounds

23

Above: *Daguerreotypes in named cases, although not rare, are less common than unnamed cases. Many of the studios employed assistants and for this reason it would be a mistake to assume that a daguerreotype bearing the name of, for example, Mayall's studio was actually taken by Mayall himself.*

Opposite, top centre: *The relatively long exposures needed for a portrait required the sitter to remain perfectly still for up to a minute and a half. To help the subject hold his position, various techniques were employed. The poses chosen were those that enabled the sitter to rest an arm on a table, or to lean against a chair, and further assistance was given by the use of clamps that held the head firmly and allowed no movement. Although exposure times were reduced as new processes were introduced, such devices continued to be used in many studios until the late 1890s.*

may well be considered reasonable. It should be remembered that examples of the daguerreotype process are not rare and the collector can afford to be selective when considering unidentified portraits of standard sizes and ignore those that show any signs of damage to the image, such as signs of rubbing or scratches. Cased or framed examples are interesting if highly decorated, or if they bear the photographer's name. Generally, however, this will only signify from which studio the item came. Many studios employed several assistants and there are relatively few daguerreotypes that can be positively identified as having been taken by a known photographer. Group portraits, exterior scenes, stereoscopic daguerreotypes and unusual subjects, such as nudes, are in demand and this will be reflected in the asking price. Value depends on rarity, and millions of daguerreotypes were produced.

Most daguerreotypists offered plates of a size suitable for mounting into jewellery and the price of these items depends to a large extent on the quality of the piece of jewellery. Although once common they are now less so, partially because they are a collectable item and also because, when purchased in the past as second-hand jewellery, the daguerreotypes were discarded. It should never be assumed that any piece of photographic jewellery is made of gold. Brass, gilt and pinchbeck were frequently used.

Of the utmost importance is the method of display and care of the collection. Daguerreotypes do not fade if exposed to light but they should not be placed in direct sunlight for long periods for two reasons. Heat will cause the mercury to sublime, or move from the plate to the glass, giving a white crystalline appearance to the inside of the covering glass, and if the image is tinted, strong light may cause the colours to fade. Leather cases may be cleaned with a leather food but care should be taken when cleaning decorated cases. Too much rubbing may remove or damage the ornamentation.

The silvered surface of daguerreotypes may oxidize,

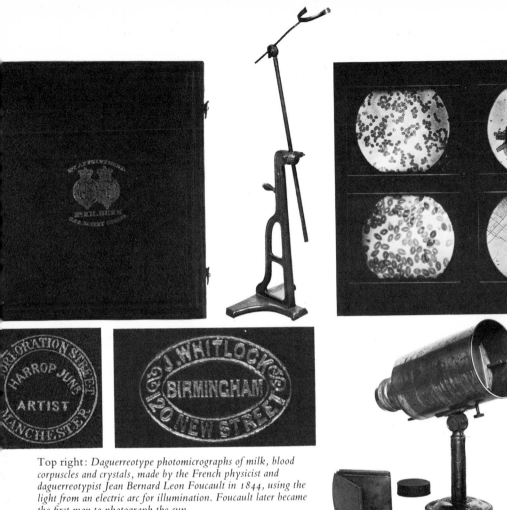

Top right: *Daguerreotype photomicrographs of milk, blood corpuscles and crystals, made by the French physicist and daguerreotypist Jean Bernard Leon Foucault in 1844, using the light from an electric arc for illumination. Foucault later became the first man to photograph the sun.*

Right: *An all-metal daguerreotype camera made by the Edinburgh optician Thomas Davidson in 1842. It is probable that Davidson only made one such example.*

resulting in a dark tarnish on the plate, and the rate at which this occurs, depends on the amount of sulphur and other impurities in the air. This is a point to bear in mind when displaying daguerreotypes in rooms with open fires. The amount of tarnish, or lack of it, is due to the effectiveness of the seal between plate and glass. From the earliest days of photography, this has been a problem with the daguerreotype process and early advertisements may be found from firms offering to clean them. The methods used were crude and highly dangerous and a collector finding a description of such methods should, under no circumstances, be tempted to experiment.

Unless the tarnish has completely obscured the image, cleaning should not be attempted. The Royal Photographic Society in London has recently prepared a paper on 'The recognition of early photographic processes, their care and preservation' which includes a section on the cleaning of daguerreotypes. This paper should be carefully studied before any

cleaning is undertaken. The general advice offered in regard to cleaning daguerreotypes is – don't. A daguerreotype will have survived for at least 120 years and may have taken the collector six months to discover. It will take him less than a minute to ruin it!

The daguerreotype was the most beautiful of all the photographic processes and the first to achieve popularity. The best examples have an affinity to the miniatures that they, to a large extent, superseded. With the ending of Daguerre's patent in 1853, there was an increase in the number of studios operating throughout the country but, by the late 1850s, the process became obsolete. The high cost of production and the absence of an effective method of making cheap copies made it unable to compete with new developments in photography.

The daguerreotype has been described as a dead-end process. It was surely the most attractive of dead ends.

Above: *An engraving by William Greatbach of John Roby, banker, organist and poet, copied from a daguerreotype by Beard. Many daguerreotypists allowed their work to be copied in this way for publication and examples are not difficult to find.*

Above: *The highly reflective surface of the daguerreotype means that it can only be viewed successfully from certain angles. By slightly tilting the image, a negative effect, so distinctive of the process, is obtained.*

Opposite, top: La Vallée des Tombeaux. *An engraving from* Excursions Daguerriennes. *One hundred and fourteen views taken from daguerreotypes were published in this series by N. M. P. Lerebours between 1840 and 1844. The original daguerreotypes would not have included figures, due to the length of the exposure times required. These would have been added by the engravers to make the pictures more interesting to the public.*

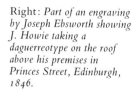

Right: *Part of an engraving by Joseph Ebsworth showing J. Howie taking a daguerreotype on the roof above his premises in Princes Street, Edinburgh, 1846.*

Above: *The back of a
sealed daguerreotype by
J. Howie of Edinburgh. A
number of daguerreotypists
put their names inside the
case and then glued the sealed
plate into the case. Attempts
to dismantle such cases often
result in damage to both case
and daguerreotype.*

Right: *Daguerreotype by J.
Howie of George Combe, the
leading phrenologist of his
day. Howie, a former painter
specializing in animal
subjects, was the first
professional daguerreotypist
to open a studio in Edinburgh
in 1841.*

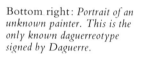Left: *The exposure time required for a half-plate daguerreotype in 1843 would have varied between 10 and 60 seconds, depending on the strength of the available light and the type of lens used. This French daguerreotype bears the remark 'Paris 1843, taken in six seconds' scratched on the back of the copper plate.*

Below: *An unusual shaped leather cased daguerreotype by Claudet measuring $2\frac{1}{2}'' \times 1\frac{3}{4}''$.*

Bottom left: *An example of an unskilled effort at restoration.*

Bottom right: *Portrait of an unknown painter. This is the only known daguerreotype signed by Daguerre.*

Below: *A photomicrograph showing part of a daguerreotype surface, taken by a scanning electron microscope giving a magnification of × 9,500. The particles of the amalgam of silver and mercury which forms the image can be seen clearly, and what appears to be a deep furrow running from the bottom left-hand corner is a minute scratch. This illustration serves to explain why the surface of a daguerreotype can so easily be damaged.*

Right: *A receipt from Mr Claudet's Daguerreotype Portrait Gallery. Such documents as bills and advertisements are of great interest to collectors.*

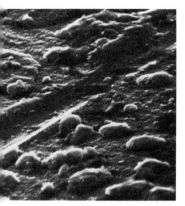

Below left and right: *In cases where tarnish has almost obscured the image, it may be worth the risk of having a daguerreotype cleaned. Results can sometimes be dramatic, but expert advice should always be sought before any attempt to rediscover the image is made. Damage to the picture cannot be rectified.*

MR. CLAUDET'S DAGUERREOTYPE
PORTRAIT GALLERY.

London _Aly 22_ 1853.

No. _20 4. 35_

The Bearer having paid £ _1_

is entitled to a _Coloured_ Daguerreotype

Portrait, No. _1_

J F Cole Clerk.

In case the first sitting should not prove successful, it will be repeated until a satisfactory Portrait can be obtained.

This Ticket will be left with the Clerk, who will give to every person a Printed Memorandum, stating in detail the amount paid for each Portrait.

Below, centre: *A sixteenth-plate (1" × 2") of a painting depicting a dead child by Ross and Thompson of Edinburgh, c. 1849. The Victorians, with their large families and high mortality rate, were no strangers to death and photographs of the 'dear departed' were mounted in mourning jewellery until the early years of this century.*

Below, right: *A quarter-plate daguerreotype (3¼" × 4¼") of an officer of the Light Company of the 2nd (Queen's Royal) Regiment, c. 1850. Photographer unknown.*

Opposite top: *A half-plate daguerreotype inscribed on the back 'John Munroe in Flairpool 1847'. Exterior scenes of this type are most unusual.*

Opposite, bottom: *A typical double-sided folding wallet case with gilt edging containing two eighth-plate daguerreotypes. Photographer and sitters unknown, c. 1852.*

Above: *A number of early daguerreotypes were encased and sealed into brass or tinned metal mounts before being inserted into leather cases. T. Wharton, who made cases for Beard in the early 1840s, usually had his name and the date of his patent, 24 August 1841, stamped on the back of the mount. Examples are uncommon, but not rare.*

Right: *A quarter-plate portrait of a Captain LeBlane in a composite moulded frame, c. 1854. This type of material was more frequently used for the manufacture of union cases.*

Left: *A quarter-plate daguerreotype in an oval mount of an unknown girl taken at Mr J. Craig's studio in Saffron Walden, c. 1853.*

Left: *Four eighth-plate daguerreotypes of young boys, probably brothers. It is unusual to find more than one photograph in the same frame, c. 1852.*

Below: *A typical sixth-plate portrait in a papier mâché frame. The sitter and photographer are unknown, c. 1850. The staining on the gilt mount could be removed by washing it in dilute ammonia, but many collectors prefer not to break the original sealing paper unless the image itself is obscured.*

Right: *A fine quality tortoise-shell case decorated with silver inlay and holding an eighth-plate portrait. Many such cases have, in the past, been adapted for other purposes, and examples with their original daguerreotypes are becoming difficult to find.*

Far right: *A fine half-plate portrait of an unknown lady by Vaillat of Lyons, 1852. The photographer's name, when known, usually appears on the case or mount. Examples on the plate itself, are fairly rare.*

Right: *Examples of various photographic processes coloured by hand. Not until the introduction of the autochrome process by the Lumiere Brothers in 1907 was a practical form of popular colour photography available.*

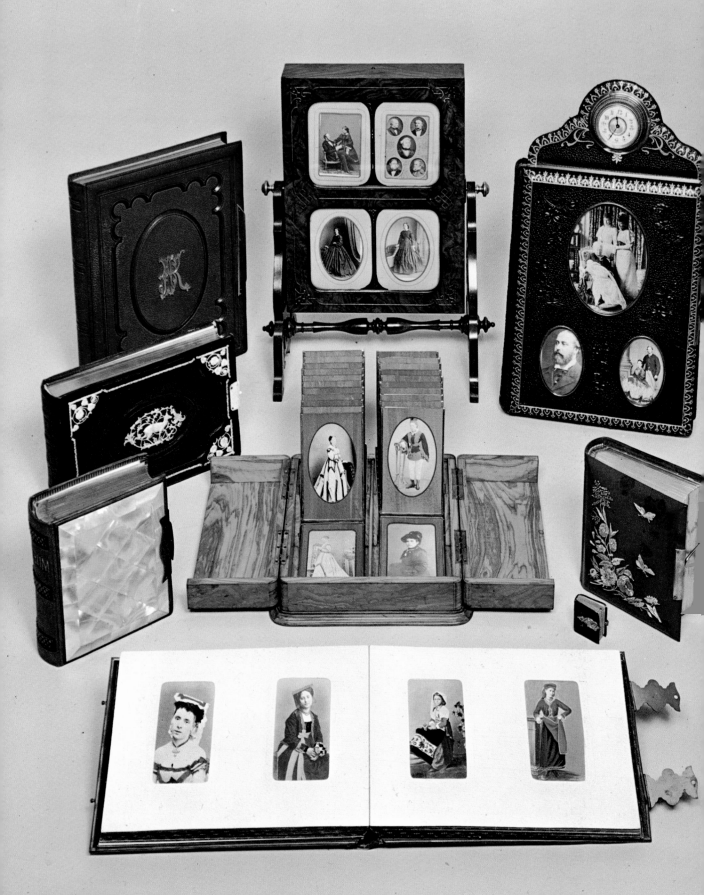

Left and below: *This quarter-plate daguerreotype of an unknown gentleman was found with a cracked covering glass in a broken papier mâché frame. Several layers of newsprint had been stuck together as packing at the back. By prolonged soaking and careful separation, part of a*

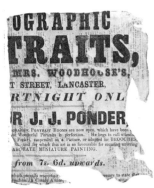

poster was found that indicates, from the date on the newspaper, that it was taken after 1849 by a travelling photographer, J. J. Ponder.
Bottom left: *A half-plate daguerreotype from the American Mid West of c. 1855. Although the process was used more extensively in America than in Europe, portraiture was the most popular subject, and fine examples of exterior views are considered highly desirable by collectors.*
Below right: *A half-plate daguerreotype showing a woman shooting. It is possible that this was a posed scene, although nothing is known of the circumstances in which the photograph was taken. On the sealing paper at the back is written 'Craigdarent 1848'. A daguerreotype of this nature is very rare.*

Left: *Seven stereoscopes in wood, papier-mâché, tortoiseshell and leather. A large number of viewers sold were designed as attractive pieces for the drawingroom, rather than as efficient optical viewers.*

Below left: *A half-plate portrait of an unknown gentleman by one of the leading American daguerreotypists, Jeremiah Gurney of New York, c. 1853.*

Below right: *From a catalogue issued by Bland & Long of London in 1854. It should be remembered that the prices quoted bear little relevance to today's values. Changing patterns of expenditure make direct comparisons impossible, but one example regarding wages may serve as a rough guide.*

In 1854, a London police constable would have received about £1.00 ($4.00) a week. The starting pay of a constable in the London area today is nearly £30 ($72.00) a week.

Right: *A fine half-plate group. On the back of the sealing paper is written 'Lt. Staples, Brigadier General Pouney, Captain Burnet, My Dear Father, Mother and myself. Taken in Captain Burnet's compound at Dum Dum artillery station, near Calcutta in February 1847'. A daguerreotype of this style and date with such information is rare.*

ESTIMATES
FOR
SETS OF PHOTOGRAPHIC APPARATUS.

(The following prices do not include a supply of Silvered Plates

DAGUERREOTYPE APPARATUS.

No. 1. Set of Daguerreotype Apparatus, for taking pictures 4¼ in. by 3¼ in., 3¼ in. by 2¼ in., and 2¼ in. by 2 in.: consisting of No. 1 walnut sliding body Camera, with single Achromatic Lens, mounted in brass front, dark slides for plates, ground focussing glass, &c.; Bromine and Iodine pans, with air-tight glass covers, and set of frames; 3 Plate Holders; 3 Plate Boxes; 2 velvet polishing Buffs; Mercury Box, with thermometer; Porcelain Washing Tray; Gilding Stand, with levelling screws; Improved Pliers; Glass Spirit Lamp; Funnel; Filtering Paper; with all the necessary Chemicals, and Polishing Materials, in hard wood boxes. The whole packed in two stained cases, with locks and handles 6

Ditto, of superior construction . . 10

If with Compound Achromatic Lens, and double Iodine and Bromine Boxes, forming a more complete set of apparatus . . . 15

No. 2. Complete set of Daguerreotype Apparatus, for portraits from 2¼ in. by 3¼ in., up to 6½ in. by 4¼ in., with best Compound Achromatic Lens, mounted in handsome brass front, rackwork adjustment; sliding body Camera of mahogany, with dark frames, focussing glass, &c.; improved Compound Iodine and Bromine Box; 2 polishing Buffs; 4 Plate Boxes; 4 Polishing Blocks; Head Rest; Mercury Box, with thermometer; Washing Tray; Gilding Stand; Improved Pliers; Spirit Lamp; Funnel and Filter Paper; Hard wood boxes, containing Polishing Materials, with all the necessary Chemicals and Materials. The whole packed in two stained wood cases, with locks and handles . . 23

Above: *A half-plate daguerreotype by an unknown photographer of an Irish street scene in Cork c. 1850.*

Above right: *A whole-plate daguerreotype of two Maori Princes with a Mr C. P. Judd. Taken by an unknown photographer in Boston, May 1850.*

Right: *A ninth-plate (2" × 2½") daguerreotype portrait of an unknown gentleman. Where the plate has a gilt frame over the paper sealing, a small suction pad can be used to remove the daguerreotype for examination. This technique should not be employed where there is no gilt frame, or the glass may be lifted from the plate and the paper sealing broken.*

Below: *A daguerreotype portrait of an unknown gentleman by Mathew Brady, c. 1855. Brady is probably best known for his photographic work during the American civil war.*

Right: *An unusually small dageuerreotype measuring $\frac{3}{4}" \times 1\frac{1}{4}"$ by H. J. Whitlock of Birmingham.*

Centre right: *A rare whole-plate daguerreotype taken in India by an unknown photographer, of Government House, Calcutta.*

Right: *A rare Australian daguerreotype ($5\frac{1}{4}" \times 4"$) of the Post Office at Beechworth, Victoria, 1857. Plate sizes vary considerably and the average collector, when describing a plate, normally takes the nearest standard size. Thus this daguerreotype would reasonably be termed a half-plate.*

Left: *A quarter-plate daguerreotype of Sir Charles Fox by an unknown photographer. Charles Fox, eminent engineer, was knighted for his contribution to the design of the Crystal Palace exhibition buildings in 1851.*

Below: *A fine vanity case given by a George Dolland Junr. to his wife on her 21st birthday in 1853. The 5" × 4" daguerreotype by an unknown photographer set in the lid is almost certainly a portrait of George Dolland. Examples of daguerreotypes in items of personal furniture of this quality are rare.*

Right: *A half-plate daguerreotype by Delemotte and Alary, May 1850. 'Ruines d'un Marallont dans l'oasis de Biskra'.*

A calotype by Dr Thomas Keith of Cardinal Beaton's house in Edinburgh, c. 1854.

3 The Calotype

The January announcements by Daguerre and Fox Talbot aroused the interest of Sir John Herschel, an astronomer and eminent scientist, who had made the discovery, in 1819, that silver salts could be dissolved by hyposulphite of soda. Although no details of the two inventions had been revealed, Herschel began his own attempts to obtain photogenic drawings and, by 1 February, was able to show Talbot the results. That Talbot was impressed by hyposulphite of soda as a fixing agent is clear from the fact that, with Herschel's permission, he wrote to the journal of the French Academy of Sciences describing the new process. The method was promptly adopted by Daguerre.

In his own work, Talbot continued to use salt as a fixing agent, having had little success with Herschel's process. By 1839, Talbot had found that if he placed one of his photogenic drawings over a freshly prepared paper and exposed it to light, he obtained a print in which the shades were not reversed. It was Herschel who named these prints negative and positive.

Talbot devoted much of his time to photographic experiments and, although his process had the advantage that from any one negative a number of prints could be made, there was no comparison with the clarity of the daguerreotype. The salted-paper prints also tended to fade if exposed to light for long periods.

In September of 1840, Talbot experimented with gallic acid. He had earlier used this substance without marked results, but in his new process the gallic acid was to prove vital. The paper was first treated in silver nitrate and then with potassium iodide, before being washed in a solution of gallic acid and silver nitrate. This method of preparing the paper rendered it far more sensitive to light than previous processes, and Talbot found that he could remove the paper from the camera before an image was visible and, by washing the paper again in a solution of gallic acid and silver nitrate, could accelerate the development of the image. After some experiments with potassium bromide, Talbot used a hot solution of hyposulphite of soda. This chemical, still in use today as sodium thiosulphate, is universally known as 'hypo'.

Talbot is said to have discovered the 'latent image' by accident whilst trying to resensitize some unsuccessfully exposed paper. To his surprise, a clear image appeared on what had been blank paper. By developing the latent image on the negatives, it became possible to obtain a photograph in a matter of minutes, as against the hour that had been needed for the photogenic drawings, and to compete with the exposure times required for a daguerreotype. For his positives, Talbot continued to use the same process that he had employed for his photogenic drawings. Indeed this method of printing out positives by daylight remained in common use throughout the last century, and printing-out paper, P.O.P., was available until recently.

In 1841, Talbot was granted a patent for his process, which he named the Calotype, from the Greek word meaning beautiful, although many preferred the name Talbotype.

The first licensee for the calotype was Henry Collen, a painter, and he exploited one of the advantages of Talbot's process. With the daguerreotype it was possible, with the use of stencil, powdered paints and gum arabic, to tint the plate, but this was the only alteration or addition that could be made. The calotype, however, could be altered in the negative or retouched on the print, and Collen made full use of this freedom to retouch his portraits. Claudet also worked with the calotype and was instructed in the process by Nicholas Henneman, who had first been employed by Talbot as a valet but, over the years, had become his assistant. Claudet, despite a great deal of work on the process and his personal appreciation of its qualities, appeared to have little success with the calotype and returned to the daguerreotype.

A number of calotypes taken by Talbot still exist and they show great skill, not only in their technical excellence, which might be expected, but also in their composition. The relaxed and casual scenes belie the care that must have been required for exposures of several minutes.

In America, despite the efforts of William and Frederick Langenheim whom Talbot had appointed his agents, the calotype was a failure. Unhampered by the restrictions of a patent, the daguerreotype had achieved such popularity that attempts to introduce the paper process met with little success.

Talbot was aware of the many uses that could be

A calotype taken at Saffron Walden, Essex in April 1858 by the Rev Edward Capel-Cure, Fellow of Merton College and Chaplain to the Queen. An amateur photographer of considerable skill, Capel-Cure used the paper negative until the late 1850s.

made of photography, not least among these being the use of his process for book illustration and, with this in mind, he opened a printing establishment in Reading in the early part of 1844. Henneman was placed in charge of the photographic work that included four major undertakings to publicize the calotype. Talbot's own book, *The Pencil of Nature*, published in six parts between 1844 and 1846, contained twenty-four calotypes, each print being stuck onto a page. This book was the first to be published illustrated with photographs, although a privately printed book had been circulated to friends earlier in 1844 by the Walters family on the death of a daughter. This book contained a single calotype of a bust of the dead girl. In 1845, *Sun Pictures in Scotland*, also by Talbot, was published with twenty-three calotypes for illustrations and a total of more than fifteen hundred

photographs were produced for Sir William Stirling's book, *Annals of the Artists of Spain*. Henneman's greatest effort, however, was in 1846 when each copy of the June issue of the journal, *Art Union*, carried a whole-plate calotype. Several negatives were used and thousands of prints were made to fulfil the order. In 1847, Talbot closed the Reading establishment and Henneman, with Thomas Malone, one of the assistants from Reading, opened a studio in London at 122 Regent Street in the following year.

The publication of so many calotypes brought the process to the attention of a wide range of the public, but unfortunately also showed one of the principal failings of the calotype. The image, if exposed to strong light for any length of time, tended to fade. It was a fault that was never completely overcome.

It was a result of Talbot asking Sir David Brewster,

A calotype by John MacCosh of the Great Pagoda at Prome, taken during the second Burma war, 1852–3. MacCosh, an army surgeon, became interested in photography in 1844 and was possibly the first British war photographer.

Principal of St Andrews University, to enquire if anyone in Scotland was interested in becoming a professional calotypist that Robert Adamson opened a studio in Edinburgh in 1843. Brewster took a keen interest in photography and introduced the painter David Octavius Hill to Adamson. The First General Assembly of the Free Protesting Church in Scotland was held in 1843, and Hill was working on a painting showing the 500 ministers who had participated. Brewster's idea was that Adamson should photograph the ministers for Hill as guides for his painting. As a result of this successful collaboration, a partnership was formed that lasted until the death of Adamson five years later.

In France, the calotype was extensively used for architectural studies and landscapes, but with little profit to Talbot, although the process had been patented in that country in 1841. Few photographers bothered to apply for a licence and Talbot's only reaction appeared to be one of irritation on learning that calotypes were being described as 'daguerreotypes on paper'.

One of the most prolific French photographers was Blanquart-Evrard who invented a new form of printing paper in 1850. Before sensitizing it with silver nitrate, the paper was coated with potassium iodide and potassium bromide dissolved in white of egg, which gave a smooth surface when dried. Albumen paper was more resistant to fading than the salted-paper prints and was soon adopted by photographers, the colour of the albumen prints being improved by the use of the gold chloride treatment after fixing.

From a printing establishment at Lille, opened by

41

Blanquart-Evrard in 1851, a large number of photographically illustrated books were produced. To reduce the time spent in preparing prints, Blanquart-Evrard used the technique employed by Talbot for developing negatives. Instead of placing a negative over a freshly sensitized paper and exposing to sunlight until the image was visible, a process that could take a long time, an exposure of a few seconds only was given. The apparently still blank paper was then soaked in a solution containing gallic acid to bring out the image. By developing the 'latent image' of each print after an exposure of a few seconds, it was possible to produce a large number of photographs in a fraction of the time required by the printing-out process. In view of the advantages of this method of developing prints, it is curious that the much more time-consuming method of printing-out remained in common use for many years.

Talbot had applied wax to his finished negatives before printing from them, thus enabling the light to pass more freely through the paper during the printing of the positives. In 1851, Gustave Le Gray introduced a variation of this process in which the paper was waxed before sensitizing. This not only improved the clarity of the image, but enabled the paper to be kept for several weeks before use, as opposed to the twenty-four hours recommended for the calotype paper, an important factor for travelling photographers.

Talbot's patent had been drawn in such general terms that further attempts to improve the process were inhibited by the fear of legal actions for infringement. In response to appeals from some of the leading scientists and photographers, Talbot relaxed his patent rights for all uses except professional portraiture in 1852. The lifting of the patent and the availability of the waxed-paper process gave a new impetus to photography. Photographic societies began to be formed, some of which still survive, and amateurs such as Dr Thomas Keith and Samuel Smith produced work of high technical and artistic quality. A considerable amount of present-day knowledge about the Victorian age has been gained from photographs taken during this period.

The young collector has little chance of acquiring calotypes by the leading exponents of the process. In London salerooms, prices for calotypes by photographers such as Fox Talbot or Adamson and Hill can run into hundreds of pounds. With patience, however, and a little study, coupled with luck, it is possible to find examples at more reasonable prices.

The first requirement is the ability to recognize a calotype, and this is not always a simple matter. Strictly speaking, a calotype is a salted-paper print from a paper negative, but processes overlap in development and use, and it is possible to find an albumen print from a paper negative, or a salted-paper print from a negative of a later process, although this is less likely. A study of the various processes for purposes of comparison should be made. Few museums have calotypes on display, and if the collector wishes to see examples, an appointment should be made with the curator. Museums are sometimes accused of being over-protective towards their collections, but it should be remembered that it is their duty to ensure that future generations can also enjoy the items in their care, and indiscriminate handling of such things as original calotypes would do little to assist this aim.

Identification of the salted-paper print is made easier by its matt finish, the surface having the roughness of good-quality writing paper of the period. On early images, the outlines may be soft, or lacking in sharp detail, as with the portraits of Adamson and Hill, although later calotypes by such men as Samuel Smith or Henry Victor Renault display a remarkable sharpness. The positive proof of the paper maker's water-

Above: *A calotype by Adamson and Hill of stone masons at work on the Scott monument in Edinburgh, 1842. The five year partnership between the two men produced about fifteen hundred photographs, many of which were portraits of well-known people. Much of their work, particularly of the men and women in the fishing villages on the East coast of Scotland, has the appearance of relaxed naturalness that is conspicuously lacking in the vast majority of daguerreotype portraits.*

Right: *A calotype of Cramond village, near Edinburgh, by an unknown photographer, c. 1845.*

mark, Turner of Chafford Mills being one, is very rare.

To identify albumen prints made from paper negatives, it may be necessary to consider other available information. Costume can often be a help in dating photographs, as can the location of a print. If found in an album filled with photographs of the 1880s, it is less likely to be from a calotype negative than if the other photographs are from the 1850s. Close examination with a lens on a part of the print where the tone is constant, may show a slightly mottled effect caused by the fibres of the paper negative. Both salted-paper and albumen prints were treated with gold chloride and possess the sepia tone this process gave. The truth of the matter is that skill in identification of photographs can only come with experience.

The recognition of a calotype negative presents fewer problems. The toning, or shading, is reversed, and the paper will have a translucent appearance caused by waxing. Sizes, as with the positives, are not standard and may vary from a couple of inches square to 10″ × 12″ and above.

It should not be assumed that all calotypes are worth great sums of money. The Victorians possessed their share of poor photographers: because only the best examples are shown in books and exhibitions, this fact is sometimes obscured.

Little can be done by the amateur to restore faded prints. All the collector can hope for is the prevention of further deterioration. Calotypes should not be stored 'image to image', but with each print separately wrapped in a paper, or inert plastic, envelope and stored flat in a folder or file. Excessive heat and dampness should be avoided at all cost.

The calotype and daguerreotype competed for public favour for fifteen years or so and, from the number of photographs taken in each process, the daguerreotype can be said to have won. Yet it was Fox Talbot's invention that led the way to modern photography.

Below: *A calotype of* The Water-seller of Saville, *an engraving by Blas Amettler from Sir William Stirling's* Annals of the Artists of Spain. *Sixty-six calotypes illustrating the work were bound in a separate volume and only twenty-five copies were issued.*

Top left: *A calotype by Fox Talbot of Magdalen Tower, from the Botanical Gardens, Oxford, c. 1842. Many photographs by Fox Talbot or his friends exist and, as his process enabled many positives to be made from one negative, it is probable that more will be found. Collectors, however, should check its authenticity with a major museum before paying large sums for a 'Fox Talbot' print.*

Above left: *An unusual paper negative with a figure inked in an upper window, c. 1850. The reversal of light and shaded areas of the subject and the often translucent effect caused by waxing, make paper negatives easily recognizable.*

Above right: *The Don Valley, near Aberdeen. An albumen print from a waxed paper negative by John Forbes White. White was introduced to photography in the mid 1850s by Dr Thomas Keith, who later became his brother-in-law. He produced a number of excellent photographs before abandoning the hobby in 1859.*

44

Below: *Eaux Chaudes, Pyrenees. A calotype by John Stewart, c. 1852. Stewart, a relative of Sir John Herschel, produced a large number of photographs, mainly in Europe.*

Right: *A calotype taken by Samuel Smith on 11 July 1853, showing the remains of* Hunstanton Hall after its destruction by fire. Smith, virtually unknown until recently, specialized in architectural subjects in the neighbourhood of his home at Wisbech. Using the paper negative process as late as 1864, he was one of the last calotype photographers.

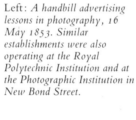

Left: *A handbill advertising lessons in photography, 16 May 1853. Similar establishments were also operating at the Royal Polytechnic Institution and at the Photographic Institution in New Bond Street.*

Above: *A calotype of the Steamboat and Railway office next to the Mitre Inn at Hampton Court by Joseph Cundell, c. 1848.*

45

Above: *Two pages
with calotypes from an
unidentified early album,
c. 1853. Before the appearance
of the carte-de-visite album,
photographs were often
pasted into scrapbooks.*

Right: *A calotype by
Adamson and Hill of Lord
Cockburn, the Scottish judge
and writer, with his family at
Bonaly Tower, Edinburgh,
1842.*

Left: *A calotype by the
American photographers
W. and F. Langenheim,
showing the building of a
lighthouse. Because of strong
competition from the
daguerreotype, Talbot's
process had little success in
America.*

Left: *A calotype of an Australian scene by an unknown photographer, c. 1852. Many experienced collectors find it curious that excellent prints by unknown photographers fetch lower prices in the sale-rooms than poor examples by known photographers. This is a fortunate trend for collectors interested in good photographs as opposed to a good investment.*

Above: *A calotype by the Rev George W. Bridges of the Acropolis from Museum Hill. Bridges was a friend of Fox Talbot and, in a letter to him from Athens dated November 1848, he wrote of having taken more than two hundred photographs in the past few months, despite difficulties in obtaining suitable paper.*

47

Above: *Rouen. A calotype
by an unknown photographer,
c. 1849.*

Left: *Agricultural machinery manufactured by Garrett and Sons. A calotype from Volume Two of* The Reports of the Juries 1851. *This four volume publication recorded the building and exhibits of the Crystal Palace Exhibition and contained 155 photographs printed by Henneman and Malone.*

Above: *A calotype by James Mudd of the exterior of the 'Exhibition House' in Manchester's Botanical Gardens, c. 1855. A former textile designer, Mudd became a professional photographer in the early 1850s and is widely known for the variety and quality of his work.*

49

4 The Wet Plate Period

In March of 1851, Frederick Scott Archer described a process that was to remain the principal method of photography for the next quarter of a century, superseding both the daguerreotype and calotype within a few years.

For an efficient employment of the negative-positive system, the support for the light sensitive chemicals had to be as transparent as possible; and glass was the obvious material. Niépce had used glass for his first successful heliographic copy of a drawing in 1822 and Herschel had taken a photograph on glass in 1839, but had found the process difficult and unsatisfactory. On the paper negatives, the chemicals had been absorbed into the fibres, and the problem with glass was to find a substance capable of holding the sensitive salts without impairing the transparency of the glass.

In 1847, Abel Niépce de Saint-Victor, a cousin of Nicéphore Niépce, had introduced a process in which the glass plate was coated with albumen and potassium iodide, and allowed to dry before being sensitized with silver nitrate. Excellent results were obtained with landscapes and art reproductions, but the exposure times of five to fifteen minutes made portraiture almost impossible. This was a serious commercial failing, for portrait photography represented a major part of the professional photographer's work.

Archer had found photography a useful aid to accuracy in his work as a sculptor, having been instructed in the calotype process by his doctor, Hugh W. Diamond, in 1847. Within a short time, Archer had begun experiments to improve the quality of photographic paper and this work led him, in 1849, to the use of a recently discovered substance. In 1847, it had been shown that guncotton was soluble in ether and produced a sticky solution that was given the name 'collodion', from the Greek word for glue. Early suggestions for its use were in the field of surgery where it was thought that its transparency when dried and its strength of adhesion, coupled with the fact that it was impermeable to water, would make it an ideal dressing for wounds.

After various experiments, Archer decided to dispense with paper and use a film of collodion as a base for the light sensitive chemicals. In 1851, he published the details of his 'wet collodion process' in the March issue of *The Chemist*. A solution of collodion and potassium iodide was poured onto a clean glass plate and allowed to flow evenly over the surface. When sufficient of the ether had evaporated to leave a tacky residue, the plate was immersed in a bath of silver nitrate. Then, whilst wet, the plate was placed in the camera for exposure and the still moist negative developed with pyrogallic acid and fixed with hyposulphite of soda. Archer's original idea had been to peel the collodion film from the plate and store it around a glass rod for fixing later, but it was found that the collodion lacked the strength for this to be practical and photographers used fresh plates for each exposure.

For the travelling photographer, the equipment required was considerable. Each stage in the preparation of the plate, as well as the exposing and developing of the negative, had to be completed before the plate dried and became insensitive to light. This meant that a dark room had to be available, and portable tents complete with chemicals, storage space for water, dishes and glass plates were soon being offered for sale. Despite the handicap of bulky and heavy apparatus, photographers quickly adopted the new process that was capable of producing negatives of high quality after exposures of only a few seconds.

For the first time in England, a method of photography completely free of patent restrictions was available for Archer had given his process to the world. For all his inventiveness and generosity, Archer received little recognition. His experiments had occupied much of his time at the expense of his profession, and for many years he had been in poor health. Some attempts were made to obtain a pension for him but these efforts met with no success, and he died in poverty aged forty-four in 1857.

Although amateurs had employed the daguerreotype and calotype processes, the cost and difficulties involved had deterred many from indulging in the art as a hobby. With the introduction of Archer's invention, photography entered into a period of increasing popularity. In 1851, there had been about a

Left: *A collodion positive on leather by an unknown photographer, c. 1855. A number of people, including Wedgwood and the Rev Joseph Reade F.R.S. had used leather in their photographic experiments, but it was probably a Liverpool photographer, C. R. Berry, who, in 1854, suggested the commercial use of leather as a base for collodion positives. Such photographs possessed the advantage of being able to be sent by post without fear of breakage. Examples are unusual.*

Above: *An excellent tintype of a Canadian Indian by an unknown photographer, c. 1860. Tintypes, first introduced in 1853, continued to be produced until fairly recently. The vast majority, however, are of poor quality and fine examples are unusual.*

Above: *An ambrotype of a street scene in Wooton Bassett, Wiltshire, dated July 1857. Photographer unknown.*

dozen studios in London and by 1866 this number had increased to 284. Photographic societies were formed throughout the world and, although many were disbanded after a few years, some still survive. Edinburgh, London, Manchester and Paris are cities that possess societies formed during this period. Books, pamphlets and manuals offering instruction and advice in all branches of photography were published, and chemists' shops began their long association with photography by stocking the chemicals required by the amateur.

One of the leading photographic dealers, Horne & Thornthwaite, advertised over forty different cameras in their catalogue for 1857, ranging in price from 9s. to £31. 9s. ($1·80–$125·80). Complete outfits containing all the photographer needed, including camera, were listed at prices from £3 to £30 ($12·00–$120·00). Portable dark tents, sold separately, were about £5 ($20·00) each.

Photography as a hobby was mainly a middle-class luxury. Wages in Victorian times were low. A skilled farm worker would have received about 10s. 6d. ($2·10) a week and, even in the cities, pay for highly regarded jobs on the railways, or in the police force as a constable, would only have been about £1 ($4·00) a week. On such wages, families could live adequately by the standards of the day, but relatively expensive hobbies such as photography were generally out of the question. However, with large numbers of studios opening all over the country and with even small villages being served by travelling photographers, the poorer section of the population could afford to have their photographs taken by a professional.

One of the popular processes used for portraiture was the wet-collodion positive, developed by Scott Archer and Peter W. Fry in 1851. Using nitric acid or bichloride of mercury, a collodion negative was bleached and placed over a dark backing or painted to give a positive effect. Although the sizes and methods of presentation were often identical to those used for the daguerreotypes, there is little excuse for the frequent confusion that arises in the correct identification of these two processes. Wet-collodion positives, or ambrotypes as they were called, lack the mirror-like surface of the daguerreotypes.

With a large number of studios competing for business, prices and quality varied considerably. Some photographers charged as little as 1s. (20 ct.), and this may have included a cup of coffee for the sitter while the photograph was being developed and fixed. Among the better photographers, prices were from 2s. 6d. to 5s. (50 ct.–$1·00) depending on the size of the photograph. Frames or cases were extra and the prices for these were influenced by the extent of local competition. For the best-quality, decorated, Morocco leather cases with embossed silk-plush linings, com-

Above: *An ambrotype portrait of an unknown lady by J. Douglas of Glasgow, c. 1856. The faint lines across the image are caused by cracks in the varnished backing. Unidentified ambrotype portraits are very common and collectors would be well advised to concern themselves only with perfect examples. This otherwise ordinary portrait is given interest by the two photographs displayed by the lady. The high reflection from the bracelet picture suggests that it may be a daguerreotype.*

Above: *An ambrotype from the American Mid West by an unknown photographer, c. 1860.*

plete with gilt mounts and glass, in a popular size of $3\frac{1}{2}'' \times 2\frac{3}{4}''$, the photographer would have paid about 9s. 6d. ($1·90) a dozen from his wholesale suppliers. These low prices applied only to the wet-collodion positives. Large portrait photographs on paper from the fashionable studios were far more expensive.

Ferrotypes, or tintypes, introduced by Adolphe Alexander Martin in 1853, were collodion positives on tinned or enamelled iron. It was a process much used by itinerant photographers, but few, if any, of the better establishments employed the method. Despite the poor quality of many of the results using this system, tintypes enjoyed a long run of popularity and were still being taken until recently by such operators as beach photographers. The finished photograph could be handed to the customer within minutes, and prices were seldom above 6d. (5 ct.).

The high sensitivity of the wet-collodion process and the brief exposures required, considerably expanded the commercial possibilities. The number of books illustrated by photographs increased, ranging in subject from poetry to travel. Francis Frith made the first of his three visits to Egypt, Nubia, Palestine and Syria in 1856 and published his work in a series of volumes that attracted much attention. Samuel Bourne, a former bank-clerk and amateur painter from Nottingham, spent several years in India and produced a large number of excellent photographs, some being taken at very high altitudes. Not until further developments had reduced the enormous amount of equipment required for such an undertaking, was this achievement equalled.

In Scotland, James Valentine and George Washington Wilson produced photographs on a commercial scale which could be purchased in albums, or as single prints. Another prolific photographer was Francis Bedford who, at the Queen's command, accompanied the Prince of Wales' entourage on a tour of the Near East in 1862 as official photographer to the party.

The realities of war were brought home to the public by photographs from the Crimea. Roger Fenton and James Robertson were prominent among the men involved in the recording of the campaign. In America, the tragedy of the civil war was documented by Mathew Brady and a team of assistants.

For the photographer wanting to produce a pictorial effect, the limitations of the collodion process could be overcome by using more than one negative to make a single print. This method, known as combination printing, was frequently employed to print cloud effects on landscape photographs. The darker foreground required a longer exposure than the sky, and consequently little detail appeared above the horizon. Two negatives were made using different

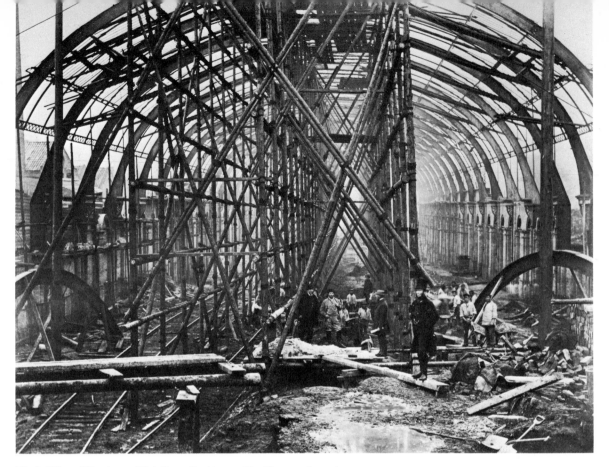

The building of Kensington High Street Station, c. 1867. Photographer unknown.

exposure times and, by combining these on one print, a complete picture was obtained. Combination printing was used with great success by Oscar Gustave Rejlander, who used up to thirty negatives to make a single print. Other photographers, such as Julia Margaret Cameron, used drapes and clever lighting, coupled with the soft focus technique, to achieve dramatic effects.

Photography was utilized by the authorities for more serious purposes. By employing the wet-collodion process for the production of Ordnance Survey maps, the Exchequer saved an estimated £30,000 ($120,000·00) a year. This fact did not appear to over-impress the Government when the subject of a pension for Scott Archer's family was being discussed. The annuity of £50 ($200·00) finally awarded was somewhat less than generous. In medicine, Dr. Hugh Diamond, the father of medical photography, photographed patients at an asylum, recording the expressions of the mentally sick. Joseph Sampson Gamgee used four prints taken by Sarony and Pierre-Petit when, in 1865, he published details of a successful operation for an amputation at the hip joint. The famous Rogues Gallery, at Scotland Yard, was begun

when prison governors were instructed in 1862 to have the prisoners in their charge photographed.

Although the wet plate process gave excellent results, it was messy, smelly and cumbersome. Photographers could be recognised by their blackened fingers caused by the use of silver nitrate. The efforts of men who recorded scenes from uninhabited areas of the world were remarkable. For any major photographic expedition, a team of porters was required to carry supplies and equipment. Stocks of glass plates, often 10″ × 12″, were no light weight and accidents on perilous mountain tracks were not uncommon.

Dry-collodion plates were available and could be purchased from photographic suppliers. Dr. Richard Hill Norris, of Birmingham, had formed the Birmingham Dry Collodion Plate Company about 1857 and achieved considerable success, but the exposure times required were longer than those needed for the wet plate. Many experiments were undertaken to overcome this problem but, before any significant results were obtained, a new process was announced that was to form the basis of modern photography.

The collector should have little trouble in learning to recognise albumen prints. The surface, unlike that

Above: *A wet collodion positive (ambrotype) with half the black backing removed to demonstrate the effect of a dark background under the bleached negative.*

Above: *An ambrotype portrait by Jabez Hogg of John Hunter M.R.C.S. taken in October 1851. The majority of ambrotypes to be found in antique shops date from after 1855, although the method of obtaining a positive image by using a bleached negative had been made public in the spring of 1851.*

of the salted-paper prints, is smooth and has a slight sheen. The sepia toning tends to be more even than that found on calotypes. Although more stable than the earlier paper process, care should be taken not to expose albumen prints to direct sunlight for long periods. If photographs are to be framed and hung on walls, it is advisable to use the more shaded areas of the room. Dirty prints may be wiped gently with moist cotton-wool, taking care not to soak the paper. For the majority of prints, it is probably unnecessary to use individual envelopes for storage, but a clean sheet of paper between each print is a good idea. Excessive heat and any degree of damp should be avoided.

With ambrotypes, there is little that can be done in the way of cleaning or restoring the image. Where the backing has become damaged, this can sometimes be replaced by a new piece of matt black paper. In many cases the backing consists of a dark varnish which may have cracked or crazed. This may be removed and a fresh coating applied. However some ambrotypes have the coat of varnish applied over the actual image, thus saving the use of a separate glass for the protection of the surface. In this situation, little can be done. Leather cases may be treated by a good hide

food. Here again care must be taken, for many of the cheaper cases were made of paper, finished as leather, and attempts to clean them will cause damage.

Prices for material from this period vary enormously, depending on the photographer and, to a lesser extent, on the subject matter. Photographs by Roger Fenton, Lewis Carroll and Mrs Cameron would be out of the reach of the modest collector in the main sale-rooms, but it is probably still possible, again with luck, to find examples of the work of now fashionable photographers at more modest prices. If the collector is interested in good pictures, often by unknown photographers, he has a good opportunity to build a worthwhile collection.

For the collector reaching the stage where he is beginning to think of specializing, he might well consider one of the two most popular forms of photography that emerged during the wet plate period. To satisfy the demand for stereoscopic images and cartes-de-visite, millions of photographs of this type were produced and sold throughout the world.

Right: *Microphotographs attached to a small lens were incorporated into a variety of articles. Generally these souvenir trinkets, containing photographs of holiday resorts, date from about the turn of the century and are fairly common. Occasionally the photographs are of a more bawdy nature.*

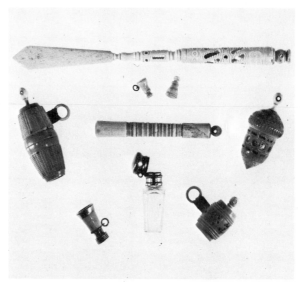

Below: *A typical wet plate stand camera by the London maker, Morley of Upper Street, Islington, c. 1865. Four silver lugs on the corners inside the plate holders prevented damage to the plate's surface during loading. Stains, caused by drops of silver nitrate from the wet glass plates, are often found on the backs of cameras of this period.*

Above: *A bracelet made from human hair with an ambrotype portrait set in a gilt mount, c. 1860.*

Right: *The execution of the conspirators involved in the assassination of President Lincoln, 7 July 1865. This picture by Alexander Gardner, a former employee of Mathew Brady, is an extreme example of a Victorian 'news photograph'.*

56

Right: *This informal ambrotype portrait was probably taken by an itinerant photographer about 1858. The relatively low prices charged for such photographs meant that photography was no longer confined to the middle classes.*

Below: *An unidentified family scene, by an unknown photographer, c. 1855. The collector with limited funds will find it difficult to compete in the leading sale-rooms for photographs by major or fashionable photographers. The story of Victorian photography, however, is not composed solely of famous names. Large numbers of amateurs enjoyed photography as a hobby and worthwhile collections from their work can be formed at reasonable cost.*

Right: *Union cases were imported into England after the introduction of Scott Archer's wet collodion process and are usually found containing ambrotypes. Those decorated with geometric designs are the most common. Cases bearing relief portraits and scenic designs are considered more desirable by specialist collectors, whilst large whole-plate sizes and small cases measuring an inch or so square are fairly unusual. Due to the brittle nature of the material, many are damaged and thus of little interest.*

Below: *Colonel Alfred Capel-Cure by his brother, the Rev Edward Capel-Cure, June 1859. Albumen print from a collodion negative. The collector who can find good photographs and then, often from only slender clues, identify the photographer, adds to our knowledge of Victorian photography as well as building an interesting collection.*

Opposite, below: *The West front of Wells Cathedral, c. 1860, by Roger Fenton. A barrister and outstanding photographer, he founded the Photographic Society of London and became its first secretary. His superb landscapes and architectural studies have been somewhat overshadowed by the fame of the photographs he produced of the battle fields of the Crimean war.*

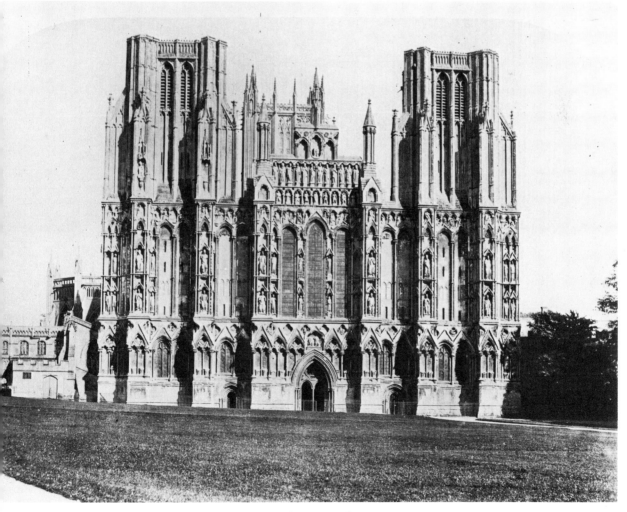

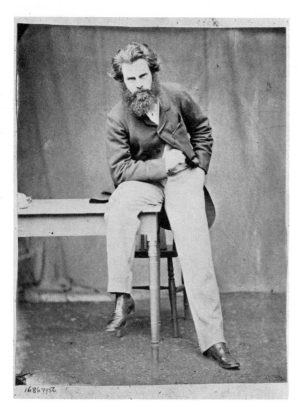

Left: *A portrait by Lewis Carroll of Thomas Woolner, the poet and sculptor, c. 1863. For more than twenty years, Lewis Carroll was an ardent amateur photographer and seldom travelled far without his camera. Carroll did little landscape photography, preferring the difficult art of portraiture. Although his photographs of young girls are well known, they form only part of the .large number of photographs he produced. Many of the 'Lions' of Victorian society as well as contemporaries at Oxford sat for him. His photographs, with their seemingly casual poses, give little indication of the care and manual dexterity required by a photographer using the wet plate process.*

Left: *A tintype of a family group on the beach at Ramsgate by F. Price. It is unusual to find the photographer's name on this type of cheap photograph.* Above: *One of Julia Margaret Cameron's portraits of Lord Tennyson. A woman of indefatigable determination and energy, Mrs Cameron was one of the great Victorian portrait photographers. Many of her photographs, which often show signs of technical imperfections, were published and sold by P. & D. Colnaghi. However, many of her other photographs display the mawkish sentimentality of the period. In fairness, it must be added that this is a minority opinion unsupported by 'experts' and rising prices.*

Above: 'In the Redan'. An
albumen print by James
Robertson taken during the
Crimean War, c. 1855.
Robertson, a former medal
designer, travelled extensively
and published photographs
from the Mediterranean,
Palestine and Syria. During
1857–8, he recorded scenes of
the Indian Mutiny. Many of
his photographs are signed.

A scene at Market Court in Kensington, London, shortly before its demolition in 1869. Photographer unknown.

Left: *A fine example of a tintype from the American civil war period. The photograph of the infantryman is marked April 1891. The photographer is unknown.*

Below: *A particularly fine example of an ambrotype taken at Niagara Falls, c. 1858. The couple posing are believed to be Senator Jefferson Davis and his wife. Davis later became President of the Confederacy during the American civil war.*

Above: *The Ordnance
Survey Photographic
Establishment at
Southampton, c. 1859,
photographer unknown. The
first floor was used for loading
the printing frames, which
were then attached to the
railing around the balcony for
'printing out'.*

Below: 'A Nor'-easter'. One of the combination prints by H. P. Robertson, c. 1870, in which the photographer used several negatives to obtain a single photograph.

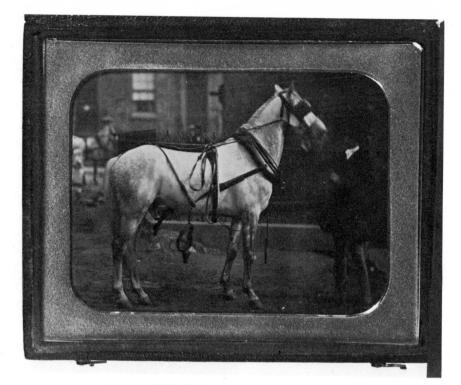

Top: *An ambrotype in a leather case of a horse and groom by the London School of Photography, c. 1853. Although many studios advertised that they specialized in equestrian subjects, such photographs are relatively unusual.*

Above: *An ambrotype of a group on an Australian Mission Station, c. 1860. Comparatively few Australian photographs appear on the English market and interesting early examples are rare.*

One half of a paper stereograph (albumen print) showing a gentleman examining a printing-out frame, c. 1854. Photographer unknown.

5 Stereoscopic Photography

Whilst visiting the Great Exhibition of 1851 at the Crystal Palace in Hyde Park, Queen Victoria admired a stereoscope and some stereoscopic photographs and thus began a craze that swept the world.

That man is able to judge distances merely by looking, is due to each eye registering a separate image from a slightly different angle. These images are received by the brain and fused into a single picture. This phenomenon of binocular vision had been known for centuries and early observers from Euclid to Leonardo da Vinci had commented on the fact.

In 1832, Sir Charles Wheatstone, an English scientist and inventor, realized that this sense of depth could be artificially induced by the use of prisms or mirrors. A London firm of opticians, Murrey & Heath, constructed a device to his specifications, and Wheatstone made two drawings, one as seen by the right eye and one as seen by the left eye. These, when viewed through the device, gave an impression of a single drawing having a third dimension. His instrument, which he named the stereoscope, was useful to demonstrate various aspects of vision scientifically but had little, if any, commercial value.

After the photographic inventions of Daguerre and Fox Talbot had been announced, Wheatstone saw the possibilities of applying these processes to his stereoscope. He commissioned Henry Collen to take two calotypes of the mathematician Charles Babbage. Each photograph had to be taken from a slightly different position and meant that the sitter had to remain motionless for several minutes. Because few people could remain without moving for so long, this method was found to be impractical for portraiture, but with inanimate objects, a splendid three-dimensional effect could be obtained. Several photographers, including Fox Talbot and Roger Fenton, produced prints for the reflecting stereoscope, which was being offered for sale by 1846 to a largely disinterested public.

Sir David Brewster, in 1849, described to the Royal Society of Edinburgh another form of stereoscope which consisted of a small box fitted with two lenses, in which two similar photographs, again taken from slightly different positions, were placed side by side.

Little interest was shown in his idea by English manufacturers, and in 1850 he took a model to Paris where Jules Duboscq, an optician, suggested some alterations to the design. It was this improved instrument that aroused the admiration of the Queen.

Following the example set by Her Majesty, the public greeted this new invention with enthusiasm. It has been estimated that, within three months, 250,000 stereoscopes were sold in England and France. This interest was directed towards Brewster's design, which had several advantages over Wheatstone's device. The new stereoscope was smaller and cheaper. A box stereoscope could be bought for as little as 2s. 6d. (50 ct.), whilst the reflecting stereoscope cost about £3. 10s. ($14·00). Due to the high degree of reflection from the surface of daguerreotypes, it was virtually impossible to use the process for Wheatstone's device, which, being open, allowed light from all angles to be reflected from the plates. In Brewster's instrument, this problem was reduced by limiting the amount of light admitted to the surface of the plate. However reflected light from stereoscopic daguerreotypes and their high cost limited their use for the stereoscope.

Once the commercial possibilities of Brewster's invention had been demonstrated, there was a rush to patent improved designs. Antoine Claudet made several important contributions. In 1853, he patented a folding stereoscope containing a stereoscopic daguerreotype. The lenses could be focussed by means of two springs. Other innovations introduced by Claudet included a cabinet stereoscope in which a number of stereoscopic pictures were mounted on an endless band. By means of knobs at the side of the cabinet, each picture could be brought into position for viewing.

Although many improvements were patented that represented some technical advance, a large number of ideas put forward served little purpose apart from attracting a public beguiled by anything described as new. The range of stereoscopes offered for sale was considerable, and designed to appeal to all tastes and incomes. The London Stereoscopic Company, formed in 1854 by George Swan Nottage, had as its slogan: 'No home without a stereoscope'. With a

A stereoscopic daguerreotype portrait of a Mrs Howard by Claudet, c. 1853. Few of the leading studios entered the business of producing stereographs on a large scale. The most popular subjects for the stereoscope were travel scenes, for which the portrait studios were not equipped.

wide range of models from 2s. 6d. to £20 (50 ct.– $80·00), the company did its best to live up to the slogan. In addition to well known companies such as Negretti & Zambra and Smith, Beck & Beck, many smaller firms made stereoscopes or ordered them from manufacturers and had their own names put on the instruments. Lenses were easily obtainable, and the simplicity of construction meant that any small firm could produce models that would sell to an eager public. Some of the stereoscopes sold during the 1850s and 1860s were somewhat ornate; more care was lavished on their appearance than on their optical qualities. The most successful of all the stereoscopes was introduced by Oliver Wendell Holmes, who complained of headaches when using the box-type viewer for any length of time. He designed a simple hand stereoscope which his friend, Joseph L. Bates, improved and manufactured in large numbers. A form of this stereoscope was still being made up to 1939.

Stereoscopic photographs, or stereographs, were produced in vast quantities, and there are no reliable estimates regarding the numbers sold. The London Stereoscopic Company alone claimed a stock of 100,000 in 1858, and they were by no means the only company in the market. The total number throughout the world could well be in the region of several million.

The examples admired by Queen Victoria were stereoscopic daguerreotypes. The process was capable of a sharpness of definition well suited to three-dimensional viewing, and many photographers, including T. R. Williams, Claudet, Mayall and Kilburn, produced them. From the commercial viewpoint, they possessed serious disadvantages. Each slide required two separate exposures, or two cameras side by side, and if several identical slides were wanted, the subject had to be re-photographed or the original plates copied in the photographer's studio. It was not a method that lent itself to large-scale production. Prices for slides ranged from 8s. 6d. to 12s. 6d. ($1·70–$2·50) each which, by the standards of the period, would be considered very expensive. Generally the subjects chosen were portraiture, usually commissioned by the sitter, or examples of sculpture and views of exhibitions. Some exterior scenes were taken, but these are now rather rare.

Although the calotype process had been used to provide prints for the Wheatstone stereoscope, few calotypes for the box stereoscope appear to have been taken. Those that are found are usually the work of amateur photographers.

In 1853, J. B. Dancer of Manchester made a camera capable of taking two pictures at the same time. This form of binocular or twin-lens camera freed the photographer from the limitations imposed by having to make separate exposures, and greatly increased the range of subjects that could be photographed for the stereoscope. Dancer's lead was followed by many other manufacturers and paved the way for the introduction of the so-called 'instantaneous stereoscopic photograph'.

It is probable that, until the 1870s, most stereo-

A stereoscopic ambrotype, showing an interior view of an unidentified church, c. 1870. The saving in cost of making the negative a positive image by bleaching and backing, rather than printing positives would appear to be the only advantage of this process for the stereoscope. No further copies could be taken and they were more difficult to view than stereoscopic albumen prints. Examples are unusual.

graphs were made using the wet-collodion process. With its high definition and brief exposures, good negatives could be obtained from which large numbers of positives could be taken. The dry-collodion plate, although having the advantage of being partially prepared, required a longer exposure and would therefore have been unsuitable for subjects where movement was likely, such as street scenes. It is impossible to tell from examination of the stereograph which process was used.

Paper prints and glass transparencies were produced to be sold at prices between 1s. 6d. and 7s. 6d. (30 ct.–$1·50) depending on quality and many suppliers graded their stereographs into four price groups. For the paper prints, the normal printing-out process was used, but for the production of glass slides, the method of printing pioneered by Blanquart-Evrard was found to be more effective. After a brief exposure, the latent image was developed and fixed. The quality of the glass slide was usually superior to the paper print and this was reflected in a higher price. The majority of stereographs were paper prints mounted on card, often with a caption and the photographer's name. Some stereoscopic ambrotypes were available but why this process should have been used is something of a mystery, as it possessed no advantage and several disadvantages.

There had been many attempts to elevate photography to an art and a few people had brought a high degree of artistry to photography. Others, such as Rejlander and H. P. Robinson, used the process to make pictures by employing several negatives to make one print, thus avoiding some of the limitations of the camera. With stereoscopic photography, there was little pretension to art; commercial success was the main purpose. Many of the stereographs were, nevertheless, of surprisingly high quality and were reviewed in the magazines of the period much as television programmes are today.

It is not difficult to understand the reasons for the popularity of stereoscopic photography. Literacy was increasing, and social conditions were improving. Railways were making travel easier, and more people had the means to take holidays away from the areas in which they lived and see other parts of their own country for the first time. For many, photography itself was a novelty, and the added attraction of being able to see the picture in three dimensions, was irresistible. It should be remembered that stereographs do not give an accurate picture of Victorian life. The beauty of the English countryside was frequently illustrated, but the poverty and derelict cottages were seldom shown. Views of Regency terraces in cities were more likely to sell than pictures of the squalor that existed in many of the industrial centres. The stereograph is as reliable as historical evidence as the picture postcard of today would be to a historian of the future.

It is possible, in a somewhat arbitrary manner, to classify the subject matter of stereographs into four main categories of travel, news, social scenes and comedy. By far the largest of these groups was con-

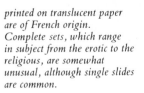

cerned with travel. Not only were large numbers of slides imported, but firms such as Negretti & Zambra and the London Stereoscopic Company commissioned photographers to travel abroad specifically to take photographs for sale in this country. At home, Francis Bedford, George Washington Wilson and J. Russell Sedgefield were among the leading photographers to produce a series of views of the British Isles.

Although newspapers carried line drawings or artist's impressions of important events, these lacked the sense of reality that the stereograph could provide. The fact that it might be several months before such a slide reached the drawing-room, tended to be overlooked by the eager purchaser.

Pictures allegedly portraying scenes of domestic or social life were intended to show an eager audience how the upper classes lived and entertained. Actors, or models, would be posed against elaborate backgrounds to simulate various social occasions. In the early 1860s, paper transparencies were introduced and much used for this type of subject. The photographs were printed on extremely thin paper and backed with another piece on which the outline of the photograph was painted in various colours. When viewed by reflected light, the picture was seen as a normal photograph but when seen by transmitted light the scene appeared in colour. A further trick was to pin-prick such features as candles or jewellery which then showed as sharp points of light when seen in the stereoscope.

Comic slides were very popular, and the style of comedy used is an indication of the class of person to whom they were designed to appeal. From the late 1850s, cheap cards began to be available in large numbers and the humour employed usually lacked any degree of subtlety and often bordered on the risqué.

By the late 1860s, the popularity of the stereograph had declined; the most common reason advanced for this was the appearance on the market of obscene slides which gave stereoscopy a bad name. A more likely explanation is that the Victorians simply became bored. It is significant that the next two periods in which the stereograph again became popular were at approximately twelve year intervals, time enough for a new generation to discover the wonders of the stereoscope. Although new processes were to widen the scope of photography and prices were to fall, stereoscopic photography never again reached the level of popularity that it had enjoyed from 1855 to 1865.

Both stereoscopes and stereographs were produced in such vast quantities that, with few exceptions, the collector can afford to reject any that show signs of damage or are poor examples of their type. When dealing with such processes as the calotype, the

Below: *A box stereoscope on a brass stand, c. 1875. The three coloured filters attached to each lens enabled the person using the stereoscope to vary* *the colour of the image being viewed. The maker of this unusual item is unknown.*

Right: *One half of a stereoscopic daguerreotype still-life showing the reflection of the photographer's studio, c. 1852. With the relatively long exposures required and the fact that a single camera was used to take the two separate photographs, still-life studies were an ideal subject for stereoscopic daguerreotypes. Although the stereograph illustrated bears the label of Carpenter and Westley, it is unlikely that the firm produced the photograph. Such slides would have been sold by a number of retailers, many of whom may have attached their own labels to the slides.*

collector may well decide that it is better to have a poor specimen than no specimen at all, but this does not apply to the subject of stereoscopic photography. Until recently, it was possible to buy large numbers of stereographs for a few pence, and even now with the increasing interest in the subject, there are few that are worth appreciable sums of money. The numbers and range of this form of photograph are so large that many collectors specialize in particular series and subjects or the work of certain photographers.

When considering the care and storage of the collection, the process involved should be the guiding factor. The same suggestions apply as already described for daguerreotypes, calotypes and albumen prints. Paper transparencies require reasonably careful handling because of the fragility of the thin paper, but otherwise should be treated as normal albumen stereographs. Glass transparencies should never be stored on top of each other. Glass tends to become brittle with age and any strain on the slide may well result in breakages. The binding on these slides is often damaged or worn and may be replaced with a pre-creased, black paper binding-tape.

Most stereoscopes were made of wood and there is always a danger of rot or worm. Unless the model is a very rare example, it is advisable not to purchase if there are signs of infestation. There are several brands of polish on the market that give some protection

against insect attack and an occasional application of such a polish is recommended. Never attempt to varnish a stereoscope. There are few things that will upset an experienced collector as much as seeing a rare stereoscope coated with a plastic sludge and brass work showing the marks of emery paper. The golden rule regarding repairs and restoration should be, if in doubt – don't.

The accurate identification of unnamed stereoscopes or stereographs is often a difficult task, due to the large numbers produced. It is hoped that this book may be of some assistance in establishing the approximate date of various items, and further information may sometimes be obtained from museums possessing photographic collections. When making such enquiries, it is sensible to send a photograph or drawing of the piece in question as mere descriptions often contain insufficient evidence on which the curator can form an opinion.

Both collectors and antique dealers would be well advised never to place a stereoscope near a window where sunlight may fall on the lenses. Several fires have already been caused by these powerful lenses acting as burning glasses.

Left: 'Damascus. The East Gate'. A stereograph and back from the series 'Views in the Holy Land' by Francis Frith, c. 1858. A number of Frith's series, including 'Views in Egypt and Nubia' and 'Views in Egypt', were re-issued several times over a period of some years and were available on card or glass.

Above right: A leather-covered folding stereoscope patented by Antoine Claudet in March 1853. These usually contain a single stereoscopic daguerreotype portrait, although some models were made with a deeper lid capable of holding a second slide behind the one ready for viewing. Similar stereoscopes were made by several firms, including Baker, Kilburn, Mascher and Mayall.

Right: An example of a fine quality cabinet stereoscope by the London Stereoscopic Company, c. 1858. This type of stereoscope, holding an average of fifty stereographs, was very popular and continued to be sold until the early years of this century.

Below: 'The Sultan's jewelled mirror and stereoscope'. Number 131 from a series of stereographs photographed by William England and published by the London Stereoscopic Company, of the International Exhibition of 1862. England was employed by the London Stereoscopic Company until 1863, and the thousands of photographs he took on journeys to America and Europe did much to enhance the reputation of the company. Later he specialized in Alpine views and published several series under the patronage of the Alpine Club.

Above: 'H.M.S. Cambridge firing a Broadside' from an instantaneous stereograph by George Washington Wilson, c. 1857. Although the exposure for this photograph must have been brief, the term 'instantaneous' in stereoscopic photography, generally referred to the taking of the two photographs at the same time with a stereoscopic camera.

Above: An advertisement by the London Stereoscopic Company, May 1856.

Left: *A box stereoscope by an unknown maker, c. 1854. This form of hand viewer is generally known as a Brewster stereoscope, after its inventor, Sir David Brewster. Very large numbers were made in a variety of styles and materials. In a much modified form, it is still available for 35mm stereoscopic photographs. Later models had lenses of a wider diameter.*

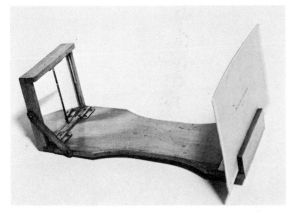

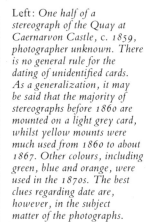

Left: *One half of a stereograph of the Quay at Caernarvon Castle, c. 1859, photographer unknown. There is no general rule for the dating of unidentified cards. As a generalization, it may be said that the majority of stereographs before 1860 are mounted on a light grey card, whilst yellow mounts were much used from 1860 to about 1867. Other colours, including green, blue and orange, were used in the 1870s. The best clues regarding date are, however, in the subject matter of the photographs.*

Above: *A variation of Wheatstone's use of angled mirrors is employed in this folding hand stereoscope of c. 1870.*

Above: *The 'Holmes' or American hand stereoscope, c. 1885. Developed from the instrument designed by Oliver Wendell Holmes in 1861, this was the most popular and efficient of all the stereoscopes. Many variations of this form of viewer were produced by several manufacturers. With a retail price of a few shillings, it remained in production until 1939.*

Left: *'The Brigade de Shoe Black' c. 1878, from a series 'Stereoscopic Views of New York' by the American photographers, E. & H. T. Anthony & Co. Founded in 1852 by Edward Anthony, a former daguerreotype photographer, the firm was one of the major producers of stereographs in America.*

898

Top left: 'Llanrwst, View from the Bridge' a stereograph from the series 'North Wales Illustrated' by Francis Bedford, c. 1862. Bedford was one of the leading producers of stereographs, both in quantity and quality. Other series issued by him include 'South Wales Illustrated', 'Chester Illustrated' and 'Devonshire Illustrated'.

Bottom left: 'Barricade dans la Grande-Rue, au Bourget'. An 1871 French stereograph by an unknown photographer. Several firms published slides allegedly depicting scenes during the insurrection in Paris, but as historical evidence they are suspect. The value of photography for the purpose of propaganda was well understood and a number of photographers, including a M. Appert, produced faked photographs during this, and later, periods.

Top right: 'Porto. Embouchure de Douro. (Portugal)'. A glass stereograph by the French firm of Ferrier & Soulier. J. Levy, c. 1867. Large numbers of high quality glass stereographs of European and Alpine views were produced by this firm during the 1860s and 1870s.

Bottom right: One of a series of stereographs taken during the building of 'The Leviathan' (The Great Eastern) by Robert Howlett and George Downes, c. 1855. Many of the early photographers issued their stereographs in series, although they were retailed as single cards.

Left: *An advertisement, c. 1855. John Charles May is described in the records of 1853 as an artist, photographer and grainer. By 1864, he had become a Photographic Artist. The fact that it was possible to hire stereoscopes and slides for an evening is an indication of the cost and popularity of stereoscopic photography.*

Right: *An advertisement for a double sided stereoscope, c. 1859. The Victorian's enthusiasm for the stereoscope was such that very large numbers of different models were produced and advertised. It is not uncommon for collectors who have specialized in stereoscopy for years to find new examples.*

YLESBURY PHOTOGRAPHIC TABLISHMENT, CAMBRIDGE-STREET.

Mr. MAY

Having erected a

GALLERY

purpose of carrying out the practice of Photography in all its , begs to state that he is now prepared to furnish **PORTRAITS**, eather, **FROM ONE SHILLING TO ONE POUND**, recent im-nts in the Apparatus and Chemicals employed rendering ght quite unnecessary. Perfect Portraits can now be taken at ablishment on Glass or Paper even during heavy rain.

copic Portraits taken at a small charge, extra on Glass or Paper, and Stereoscopic Views to order.

opes and Slides in great variety, also lent out for the Day or Evening on moderate terms.

raphs of Fat or Prize Cattle taken, and Painted afterwards on a large scale if required.

zed Collodion, Positive or Negative, 9d. per ounce. J. C. Bromo-Iodized Composite Collodion for Positives, warranted to od for Months, 1s. per ounce. Developing and Fixing Solu-the above, 1s. and 1s. 6d. per pint, and all other Photographic als of the greatest purity.

R. GIBBS, PRINTER, ADVERTISER-OFFICE, AYLESBURY.

Left: *One half of a stereoscopic daguerreotype showing part of the Museum of the Royal College of Surgeons, taken in the summer of 1852 by Lebeau. Several examples of this stereograph are known and it is possible that the slide was available for sale to the public.*

Above: 'The Wearer and the Maker'. A stereograph showing the Wearer in a comfortable room whilst the Maker sits in her garret, c. 1859, photographer unknown. It is rare to find a card of this period suggesting a social comment.

Top right: One of the twenty stereographs contained in Charles Piazzi Smyth's Teneriffe, the first book to be published using stereographs as illustrations. In 1865, Smyth photographed the interior of the Great Pyramid.

Left: About 1890, companies like The Keystone View Co., H. C. White & Co., and Underwood & Underwood published huge numbers of stereographs. Attractively boxed and sold worldwide, these American companies dominated the last period of the stereograph's popularity.

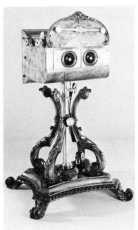

Above: An ornate stereoscope by Hirst and Wood of Huddersfield, c. 1862. Stereoscopic photographs on card mounts could be viewed by light reflected from a mirror attached to the underside of the lid. With the lid closed, glass or translucent paper stereographs were viewed by light through a ground glass screen at the back. An additional feature was a roll of coloured gauze which wound behind the paper

slides to change the background colour. The author's failure to find an example leads him to call it rare.

Above right: Swan's Crystal Cube, or Casket Photograph. A pair of stereoscopic collodion positives were mounted on two prisms in such a manner that a single stereoscopic image was seen when viewed from a certain angle. Swan's idea was patented in 1862.

Above: A stereographascope or combination viewer, c. 1860. This type of stereoscope, combining a large convex lens for the viewing of prints, was very popular and remained in production for many years. First introduced in the early 1850s, many variations of this model were available. The example shown is perhaps one of the more unusual forms.

Right: A 'Wheatstone' reflecting stereoscope by Horne and Thornthwaite, c. 1857. The lensless eye piece allows a limited field of vision to the angled mirrors in which are reflected the photographs. The pictures are fused into one three-dimensional image by the brain. Examples are rare.

Right: 'Orton's Fish Balloon, Ascent from Crystal Palace, July 11th 1870'. Charles Breese, a Birmingham photographer, whose London studio was at Sydenham published a series of high quality glass stereographs at 5s ($1.00) each. He also produced a number of 'special copy' slides, of which 'Orton's Balloon' is one; these sold at £1.1s ($4.25) each. This photograph, however, has been faked, for the balloon is painted on the inside of the covering glass. Enlarged section of Charles Breese's faked slide, showing the painted-on balloon.

Below: 'The Orphan's Dream' c. 1857. Sir David Brewster first suggested the use of a partial exposure to create the illusion of a spirit figure. The ghostly effect was obtained by allowing the model to remain in front of the camera for only a second or two. This type of photograph, now found amusing, was not thought so then. In 1858, a reviewer complained that it did not possess all the poetical feeling that the subject demanded.

Above: A family scene, c. 1859, photographer unknown

Bottom, centre: Aylesbury, c. 1855, photographer unknown. Although most nineteenth century stereographs were commercially produced, some were taken by amateurs. Several clubs existed for the exchange of slides between enthusiasts, and examples that can be identified as having been taken by a member of such a club, are of interest.

Centre, right: A rare stereoscopic daguerreotype showing the building of the extension to Paddington Station, London, 1852. Photographer unknown.

Above: One half of a stereo pair showing the making of stereographs, c. 1860. Photographer unknown.

A PRESENT TO AN OLD BACHELOR.
Copyright.

AN OPTICAL DELUSION.—THINGS SEEN, AND THINGS NOT SEEN.
Copyright.

A NICE REFLECTION.
Registered.

J. BLAKE, PHOTO.　　　DEVONPORT

J. BLAKE
PHOTOGRAPHER
93, FORE STREET,
DEVONPORT

COPIES OF THIS PORTRAIT MAY BE HAD ON APPLICATION.

R. Jenkins
Smoke Apparatus

6 Cartes-de-Visite

The most popular form of photograph in the nineteenth century was doubtless the carte-de-visite. If the collecting of stereoscopic photographs could be described by contemporaries as a craze, then the Victorians' enthusiasm for the carte-de-visite amounted to little less than mania.

The identity of the first man to suggest pasting a small photograph on a card mount and using it as a visiting card, is somewhat uncertain. Several photographers in different countries have been credited with – or claimed credit for – the idea, but it is probable that a French photographer, Louis Dodero, was the first to describe the format. In a letter to the journal *La Lumière,* on 24 August 1851, he also proposed that photographs should be attached to passports and other official documents. It was, however, some years later that another French photographer, André Disdéri, who, realizing that he could reduce his costs by taking several negatives on a single plate, introduced the fashion commercially and was responsible for its popularization.

In the early 1850s, a 10″ × 8″ portrait photograph on paper could cost £2–£3 ($8·00–$12·00) and, if the photographer was well-known, the charges were even higher. Prices of this sort meant that photography was far beyond the reach of ordinary people, the majority of whom earned less than £1 ($4·00) a week, and it was to this market that the carte-de-visite was directed. Cameras and sliding-plate holders were designed to take several of the $2\frac{1}{4}″ × 4″$ carte-size images on one plate, and photographers began turning to this lucrative source of business. There was some competition from the ambrotype and tintype but, as these were direct positive processes, the carte possessed the advantage that copies could be purchased for less than the cost of the original photograph.

It took a few years for the public to accept fully the new form of photograph but, by 1860, the demand was so great that not even the leading and fashionable studios could afford to ignore the business opportunities. Beard, Claudet, Kilburn, Mayall, Rejlander and T. R. Williams were among the established photographers to produce cartes. Other men without much knowledge of photography, but tempted by the money to be made, opened studios and hoped for the best. In many cases, their customers were delighted with what may have been the first likeness of themselves they had owned. The carte-de-visite was the first popular form of portrait photograph that appealed to all classes. Because of their cost, daguerreotypes and calotypes had been limited to the more prosperous sections of the community. With prices of 12s. 6d. ($2·50) for a dozen, and sometimes even less, there were few who could not afford a visit to the photographer's studio. Many of the photographs taken possess little merit. Due to the low prices and constant stream of customers, there was hardly any attempt to produce originality in the portraits, and the work of many of the cheaper operators was a succession of uninspired stereotyped images.

For the more discriminating, there were studios that sought to rise above the level of mere image recorders. Disdéri's studio in Paris, sumptuously decorated and staffed by more than eighty assistants, catered for about two hundred sitters a day, and, by the mid-1860s, he had extended his operations to England and Spain. It would almost be misleading to describe Camille Silvy's London establishment in Porchester Terrace as a studio, for it was luxuriously furnished with antiques, tapestries and sculpture. It proved to be a sound investment for, after ten years of photographing fashionable society, Silvy was able to retire in comfort. A large number of other studios produced work of high quality but, of the thousands throughout the world, they were in a minority.

The use of painted backgrounds had been pioneered in the 1840s by Claudet and, with the introduction of the carte-de-visite, the production of backcloths and studio props became a minor industry. Most photographers had only one or two studio sets. The camera would be already focussed on the position in which the customer would be placed and the plate exposed. Even the angle of the subject's head might be predetermined by the amount and direction of the available daylight. For the more ambitious studio, there was practically no limit to the background situations that could be created. Long backcloths on rollers were turned to give a selection of painted scenes

Above left: Three examples of comic cartes-de-visite, c. 1865, possibly by the London Stereoscopic Co. Negatives taken for the production of comic stereographs were sometimes used for this type of carte. Left: A cabinet photograph of the smoke apparatus invented by Chief Boatswain Richard Jenkins of the Royal Navy. This photograph may have been taken when Mr Jenkins applied for a patent in January 1880.

A typical example of art work on the back of a cabinet
photograph.

and, with a number of stage props before a suitable
background, anything from a hunting scene to a
bridge of a ship could be provided.

The name 'carte-de-visite' is, of course, the French
term for a visiting card; although this name remained
in general use, there is no evidence to suggest that
they were ever used for this purpose. In any case, the
custom of leaving cards was very much a middle-class
convention, and most people of that class throughout
the world would have regarded the leaving of a
photograph as a trifle vulgar. In one sense only did the
carte become a visiting or, to be more accurate, a
trade card. The backs of the cartes were used by
photographers to advertise their studios. Many of
these elaborate advertisements with their art work of
cherubs and scrolls also listed other photographic
services offered, which can be of interest to the modern
collector.

It is more than probable that, if Queen Victoria and
Disraeli had strolled arm in arm along the High Street
of any provincial town in the mid-1850s, the fact
would have been unreported, for the simple fact is
that, until the coming of photography, the faces of the
country's leaders were virtually unknown to the
public at large. The carte-de-visite did much to change
this. Almost every individual of note, from Her
Majesty to minor authors, was persuaded or paid to sit

for their portrait, and the cartes of well-known per-
sonages sold by the thousand. Large amounts of
money could be made by photographers who chose
their subjects well. Mayall is reported to have received
the staggering sum of £35,000 ($140,000·00) for his
portraits of the Royal Family, and the most popular
picture of all is believed to be one of the Princess of
Wales carrying her child, Princess Louise, on her back.
This photograph by W. D. Downey is said to have
sold more than three hundred-thousand copies.

Not all the portraits of famous people bore the name
of the sitter, and the collector often comes across a
photograph of a familiar face which he cannot identify.
Some personalities were portrayed several times by
different photographers, and it is sometimes difficult
to recognize any similarity in the images. Other subjects, although well-known at the time, have now
slipped into obscurity.

The carte, like the stereograph, served to some
extent as a news photograph. For a few years, the
Tichborne case fascinated Victorian England and
cartes of the main characters in the affair were offered
for sale. Athletes, bishops, actresses and members of
the nobility lay side by side on the shop counter.
Leading figures in public life were judged by photographers, not for their virtues or vices but for their
ability to be good sellers. Many museums, particularly

An unusual photographic representation of the death scene of the Prince Consort, created by Leopold F. Manley of Portman Square and published as a carte-de-visite by J. W. Smith of Baker Street, London. This is another example of the combined work of the photographer and artist.

the National Portrait Gallery in London, are now building up collections of cartes of the men and women who made the Victorian age such an outstanding period.

Cartes-de-visite continued to be produced until the early years of this century, but their popularity had begun to wane in 1866 when a new size was introduced. Measuring $5\frac{1}{2}'' \times 4''$, the 'cabinet' photograph soon won the public's approval, but their interest never reached the level of the enthusiastic acclaim that had been accorded to the carte in its heyday.

Cabinet photographs were, in effect, a larger version of the carte-de-visite and although, by virtue of the increased size, portraits of greater detail were possible, many collectors find that they lack the charm and appeal of the early cartes. There were marked differences in the choice of subjects for the cabinet. Comic scenes, which had featured on many cartes, were seldom taken, and the commercial portraits offered for sale tended to be mainly of actors and actresses. Photographers again used the back of the mount to advertise themselves and with more space available, their designs became even more ambitious. Many otherwise indifferent cabinet photographs are well worth collecting for the delightful absurdities of the art work.

Unlike the daguerreotype and ambrotype, the

surface of the carte required no covering glass for protection, and the production of cases for photographs declined sharply. Paper prints had been kept in scrapbooks and albums since the 1840s, but with the introduction of photographs mounted on cards of a standard size, manufacturers began producing albums specifically for them. The most common form of album was usually bound in embossed leather with a tooled spine. The pages were frequently decorated and contained up to four apertures into which the cartes were slotted.

For the buyer who was willing and able to pay more, there was a bewildering range from which to choose. Velvet, carved wood, silver, ivory and mother-of-pearl were only some of the materials used for albums. Many had gilt clasps and some could be locked. Others contained musical boxes which played when opened. In the 1870s, revolving albums holding up to sixty photographs were marketed. By a simple method of sliding frames, the four cartes on display could be changed by turning the album on its axis. Large wooden fans, each section containing a carte, could also be purchased.

As the cabinet photograph gained in popularity, so albums able to take the new size appeared in the shops. It is, however, a mistake to assume that an album designed only for cartes must have been made

Six cartes-de-visite by Camille Silvy.

before 1866, for such albums continued to be advertised and sold until after the turn of the century.

For the young beginner, cartes and cabinets offer a possible area of Victorian photography in which to specialize. Despite rising prices, the majority of cartes can still be bought for a few pence each, and such were the numbers produced that the collector might well be advised to narrow his interest to just one or two types, such as the topographical scenes by photographers like Francis Bedford or portraits of well-known people. There is a wide variety of subjects from which a choice could be made.

The same methods of care that were suggested for the albumen prints and card stereographs, also apply to cartes. If attempts are made to clean the images with moistened cotton-wool, it should be remembered that the photographs were stuck on the card mounts with water-soluble glue and too much moisture will lift the print from the card. No attempt should be

made to clean the back of a carte with water. A piece of dry bread or a very soft rubber lightly applied is usually effective.

A point that will have to be considered sooner or later is the question of preparing a catalogue of the collection. It may be unnecessary to list rare items such as calotypes, as with their scarcity it is unlikely that many will be acquired, but with stereographs, cartes and later prints, numbers can mount up surprisingly quickly. It is advisable, therefore, to begin some form of record before it becomes a major task.

In these days of rising crime rates, it is a sensible precaution to photograph the more valued items in your collection. At least one owner recovered her collection after a burglary by distributing copy photographs among fellow collectors and, as a result, three men were arrested by the police.

E. E. J. M.
Home for Working & Destitute Lads.

No. 27.—ONCE A LITTLE VAGRANT.
(The same lad as on card No. 28.)

E. E. J. M.
Home for Working & Destitute Lads.

No. 28.—NOW A LITTLE WORKMAN.
(The same lad as on card No. 27.)

Two cartes, c. 1874, from a series published by the East End Juvenile Mission, later to become better known as Dr Barnardo's. To raise funds and publicize the work being undertaken at the mission, cartes were sold at 6d (10c) each or sets of twenty for 5s ($1.00). By 1874, the mission had established its own studio at Stepney.

"CARTE DE VISITE,"
20 for 20s.

hotographed by an Eminent Foreign Artist in
a most superior style.

NDON STEREOSCOPIC COMPANY,
54, CHEAPSIDE, LONDON.

tention 3 Minutes.   Albums from 12s 6d. each.

Above: An advertisement for cartes-de-visite by the London Stereoscopic Company, c. 1861. As the sale of stereoscopic photographs declined, the company diversified into other forms of photography. Examples of cartes by the London Stereoscopic Company are common.

ADAMS & CO.'S STUDIO CHAIRS.

THESE are the very finest upholstered chairs obtainable. We are Determined to supply the very BEST goods only at the LOWEST prices. In plain crimson or figured velvet of any colour. All subject to our usual 5 per cent Discount for cash with order.

No. 1.—4 Backs, £7 5s.

Above: An advertisement of 1891 by Adams and Company. A number of firms specialized in the business of supplying furnishings for photographic studios. Many of the articles used in the studio would have been of little use in a home. Tables were made with legs of different styles at each end so the photographer, by turning the table, had two props for the price of one. Examples of early studio props are rare.

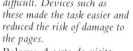

Above left: *An unusual memorial carte-de-visite by John and Thomas Spencer, 1865.*

Above: *Samuel Palmer, the painter; a carte-de-visite by the London photographers, Cundall Downes & Co.*

Left: *Lund's photographic forceps, c. 1880. The insertion and removal of cartes from the slotted pages of albums could be quite*

difficult. *Devices such as these made the task easier and reduced the risk of damage to the pages.*

Below: *A carte-de-visite viewer, c. 1862. These small wooden boxes with a lens in the lid by which cartes could be examined, were produced in large quantities.*

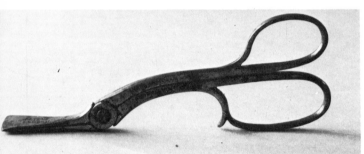

Left: *A page from a scrap book showing a painting of an album on which two carefully cut photographs have been pasted. Scrap books in which photographs have been pasted on decorated pages are unusual, although not always of great value.*

Right: *A miniature album measuring $\frac{3}{4}'' \times 1''$ in tortoise-shell inlaid with gold and silver, c. 1875. Most examples found are dated c. 1900 and include souvenir items in cheap metal.*

Above left and above:
*Two cartes-de-visite of
employees of the British
Plate Glass Company at
Ravenhead, St Helens,
from an album originally
owned by John Crossley,
co-partner and manager of the
company, c. 1867.*

Above: *A musical album
sold by Acton Griffiths of
Baker Street, London, c.
1865. Although such albums
are common, it is unusual to
find one in perfect condition.
The example illustrated is
unusual in that the musical
box is concealed behind the
spine of the album.*

Left: *A carte-de-visite by
the London School of
Photography showing an
unknown gentleman, c. 1861.
The base of the head rest
normally used to support the
subject is concealed in this
photograph by the carefully
draped curtain.*

87

Top: *Three cartes-de-visite from Disderi's Paris studio, c. 1862.*

Above left: *A carte of an unknown gentleman by the London photographer Alexander Bassano, c. 1860. Cases, which had been necessary for the protection of the delicate surfaces of the daguerreotype and ambrotype,* continued to be used for a time by some photographers as a means of presentation for the carte-de-visite.

Right: *A number of photographers, both English and foreign, issued cartes-de-visite of members of the Royal Family that sold in large numbers. The composite carte illustrated was probably produced by Mayall.*

Left: *A large and ornate table album with a sculptured metal decoration on a green plush base, c. 1870. Little can be said about this Victorian monstrosity, except that the author likes it.*

Right: *Another carte-de-visite of an employee of the British Plate Glass Co. Photographs from this period, recording the costumes and specific occupations of industrial workers are rare.*

Below: *A portrait of Queen Victoria, c. 1863, possibly by Mayall, superimposed on an 1817 engraving of a staircase at Buckingham House and published as a carte-de-visite.*

Below: *A cabinet photograph of a gentleman and his Penny-Farthing. This photograph not only illustrates the use of an elaborate studio set, but also demonstrates how otherwise indifferent portraits can be of value as a record of the life and pastimes of a vanished society.*

Above left: *A composite carte-de-visite photograph of some of the leading Victorian scientists in which photographic portraits have been combined with art work.*

Below left: *A 'Medallion Portrait' was but one of the many names used by enterprising photographers to add a touch of novelty to cartes-de-visite. The example shown is of interest because the photographer, Mr John Thomas, used a portrait of himself to advertise his Cambrian Gallery in Liverpool.*

Above right: *Although many of the larger studios employed their own colourists to tint photographs, independent artists, such as Mr W. M. Thompson, could make a reasonable living by offering their specialized services to both the public and the trade.*

Below right: *A page from a carte-de-visite album containing portraits of Fellows of the Royal College of Surgeons, photographed by Moira & Haig of London, c. 1865.*

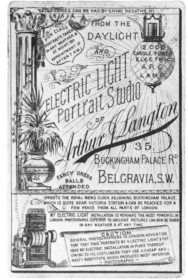

Above left: *A carte-de-visite by James Valentine of Sir David Brewster, c. 1860. Valentine was a Scottish landscape photographer who later employed a considerable staff and photographs bearing his name or initials are not difficult to find. Cartes and stereographs by Valentine are less common.*

Above right: *The majority of Victorian portraits were taken* in studios lit by daylight. Some enterprising photographers were quick to take advantage of new light sources. Both gas and electricity were used; probably more for their novelty value than efficiency.

Below: *The popular pastime of collecting cartes-de-visite of the Royal Family was sometimes exploited for commercial purposes.*

H.R.H. THE DUKE OF EDINBURGH.

(Copyright.)   SEE OVER.

114 TEMPERANCE
BUCHANAN'S TEETOTAL COFFEE & REA
BUCHANAN'S TEMPERANCE HOTEL

7 The Dry Plate

From 1851, Scott Archer's wet-collodion process dominated photography, although dry plates were available that reduced some of the inconveniences and difficulties faced by photographers. The Birmingham Dry Collodion Plate Company had been formed about 1857, the Liverpool Dry Plate Company was formed in 1867, and a number of photographic stockists offered plates of their own manufacture, but many photographers considered that the saving in labour offered by the dry processes, was offset by the longer exposures that these plates required.

One of the more successful dry processes using collodion and albumen, was invented in 1855 by J. M. Taupenot, a French chemist, and used by many photographers including James Mudd and Robert MacPherson. These plates could be kept for several weeks before use, but needed exposures six times longer than required by the wet plate. The difficulty lay in the fact that, once the collodion had been allowed to dry, chemical changes occurred that rendered it less effective as a base for the light-sensitive salts.

Some of the materials experimented with to overcome this problem suggest a degree of desperation. The use of such ingredients as sugar, beer, tea, sherry, treacle, honey, ginger wine and vinegar has prompted one leading photographic historian to refer to the 'culinary period of photography'.

It was poor health that made Dr Richard Leach Maddox, a general practitioner, seek an alternative to the wet plate. He was a keen microscopist and used photography in his experiments, but found that the smell of collodion caused him acute discomfort. After a great deal of work, and a number of failures, he published a process on which modern photography is based. In the September issue of the *British Journal of Photographer* in 1871, Maddox described how cadmium bromide and silver nitrate could be mixed in a solution of gelatine to form an emulsion of silver bromide. Within two years, plates coated with a gelatine emulsion were being advertised, but without much success.

In 1874, Richard Kennett, an amateur photographer, marketed a dried gelatine emulsion that the customer could reconstitute with water. Plates made by this method were more sensitive than those described by Maddox and another amateur photographer, Charles Bennett, realized that the cause of this lay in the effect of the heat used to dry the emulsion. On 29 March 1879, he published in the *British Journal of Photography* a method of 'ripening' the gelatine emulsion by cooking for long periods and thus considerably increasing its sensitivity.

The dry plates using this new process needed only a tenth of the exposure times required by the wet plate and, at last, the photographer was free of the cumbersome equipment that had been necessary for so long. Until 1878, photography had demanded some knowledge of photo-chemistry and a degree of manual dexterity in addition to an eye for a good picture. Now, however, only a camera and a packet of plates were needed. After exposure, the plates could be kept for development later. By the end of 1879, there were more than fourteen firms producing dry plates for an expanding market.

One of the effects of the introduction of a fast process was the change brought about in the design of cameras. With long exposures, it had been the practice to estimate the time needed and remove the lens cap for the necessary period, but, with exposures of a twenty-fifth of a second or less, more accurate methods of timing were essential. Shutters, capable of working at these relatively high speeds, were produced and fitted to lenses. Another important development resulting from the shorter exposures, was the production of smaller cameras that could be used without being fixed to a tripod.

Eadweard Muybridge, an English photographer working in America, took a remarkable series of photographs with gelatine plates in the 1870s. His pictures, showing in detail the actions of men and animals in motion, were published in *Animal Locomotion* in 1887. By employing several cameras placed at set distances alongside a race track and stretching strings across the track attached to shutter control mechanisms, Muybridge obtained a high-speed photograph of a race horse with all four feet lifted from the ground at the same time, thus settling a long argument between artists and sportsmen. Muybridge's

Left: A street scene by the Edinburgh photographer Balmain, showing Thomas Simpson, better known as Coconut Tam, a well known character in the city during the 1880s.

93

work was to have a direct influence on the introduction of cinematography in the 1890s.

Just as Scott Archer's invention had widened the range of photography in 1851, so the availability of a fast and reliable dry plate further extended the activities of photographers. Much of the formalized style of the wet plate period had been dictated by the limitations of the process and, with the advent of almost instantaneous photography, there was a movement to exploit the opportunities offered by the new techniques. Dr Peter Henry Emerson, an East Anglian writer and photographer, exercized considerable influence with his naturalistic photographs which were in marked contrast to the contrived artificiality that had been favoured earlier. The freshness of this new approach was typified by the work of Frank Meadow Sutcliffe, who opened his studio at Whitby in Yorkshire in 1875.

As the demand for photographically-illustrated books continued to rise, the use of individually printed photographs became progressively more impractical. From the mid-1870s, one of the most beautiful permanent processes for reproducing photographs was used with great success for many publications. The woodburytype, patented in 1864 by Walter Bently Woodbury, was produced by using an original negative to make a relief in bichromated gelatine. This relief was then forced, under pressure,

against a lead plate to form a mould, which could be filled with coloured gelatine for printing up to 120 copies an hour.

The woodburytype could be produced in large numbers at a low cost per print, but still had to be stuck on the pages by hand. In the 1880s, the halftone process, by which the image was reduced to a series of dots for mechanical printing on the page – an idea first suggested by Fox Talbot in 1852 – came into use and, by the 1890s, the woodburytype was obsolete.

The large numbers of cameras of different designs that were being offered for sale in the 1880s reflected the enormous interest in photography. For the amateur, it was still a hobby that required some dedication. Cameras remained expensive, and the availability of a dark room for developing negatives was essential. Although the amount of the necessary apparatus had been reduced by the invention of the dry plate, the camera, tripod and supply of glass plates, which could measure up to $15'' \times 12''$, were no light weight if they had to be carried for long distances.

In 1884 the Eastman Dry Plate Company, which had been formed by George Eastman in America in 1881, introduced the Eastman Negative Paper. Using paper to carry the gelatine emulsion, instead of bulky and fragile glass, proved popular. Eastman, realizing the potential of the market, continued his experiments and, in 1885, announced a new process in which the paper

A sequence of photographs of a dog walking, by Eadweard Muybridge, 1887. Muybridge's work in the analysis of movement by photography led ultimately to the introduction of cinematography in the 1890s. In addition, Muybridge published many stereographs, magic lantern slides and conventional photographs. Examples are more readily found in America.

Far left: *A typical field camera of the dry plate period manufactured by Adams and Company, c. 1885.*

Left: *The Brownie camera, 1900. The first of a generation of cheap cameras to bear the name 'Brownie', this simple roll film camera sold for 5s ($1.00) and brought photography within the reach of all but the very poor.*

Left: *The first photographic magic lantern slides were produced in the 1850s, but most examples found will be from the dry plate period. Subjects range from the commercially-produced narrative series to holiday photographs taken by amateurs.*

served only as a support and was removed after the sensitive gelatine layer had been processed. As the business of his company expanded, Eastman, no longer able to devote enough time to experimental work, engaged Henry M. Reichanbach, a chemist, to find a substance that would combine the flexibility of paper with the transparency of glass. Reichanbach turned his attention to cellulose nitrate and, after three years' work, produced a form of this material that was suitable as a carrier for the emulsion. The Eastman Transparent Film, patented in December 1889, provided the transparency and flexibility that Eastman had wanted, and went into production in the summer of 1889.

The name 'Kodak' first appeared in 1888, when Eastman designed a camera to take his paper-backed rollfilm. It was a camera designed for the novice. Loaded with enough film for 100 exposures, it fulfilled the advertising claim of 'You press the button, we do the rest'. When the owner had pressed the button 100 times, he posted the camera to the factory where his photographs were developed, printed and returned to him with the camera reloaded with another roll of film.

Despite the simplicity of operation and the brilliance of Eastman's sales campaign, the cost of £5. 5s. ($21·00), plus £2. 2s. ($10·40) for developing and reloading, meant that photography was still too

expensive for the majority of people. Several successful cameras, including folding models, bearing the name Kodak were marketed during the next twelve years, but it was not until 1900 that the first of the famous, cheap, Brownie box cameras appeared. One hundred years after Wedgwood had begun his experiments to capture Nature's images, the man in the street was able to buy a reliable camera for 5s. ($1·00).

Many collectors, although valuing the work of Sutcliffe, Paul Martin, Sir Benjamin Stone and other leading photographers of this period, tend to ignore snaps by unknown amateurs. This is a pity, for historians of the future may well place more reliance on this type of photograph than on those taken for their pictorial interest.

There is always a temptation, when starting a collection, to buy anything that is offered, regardless of condition. The result of indiscriminate buying is liable to be a pile of unrelated items of little interest and less value. In a book addressed to collectors, it may be out of place to suggest that expert opinion on what to collect should be mainly disregarded. The majority of photographic collections of interest were built up by people who bought what they liked, regardless of the fact that the subject was unfashionable and totally ignored by everyone else. Information and advice can be invaluable, but the final choice of subject must belong to the collector himself.

Above: *A view of the printing section of G. W. Wilson's establishment at Aberdeen, c. 1884. Until the end of the century, most printing – even on the large scale required for commercial production – was done by daylight.*

Right: *A caricature by Spy of Sir Benjamin Stone, the politician and well known photographer. Posters, cartoons and caricatures relating to photography are of interest and some collectors specialize in this aspect of the subject.*

Far right: *Whitby Harbour, 1904. A photograph by Frank Meadows Sutcliffe.*

96

Far left: *High Street, Falkland in Scotland by G. W. Wilson, c. 1886. Francis Frith and James Valentine also produced prints on a large scale. Their photographs can be identified either by their names or initials.*

Left: *A photograph taken for the grocery firm of J. Sainsburys, showing their premises in Chapel Street, North London, c. 1890.*

Right: *Photographs on ceramics, enamels and glass ware are not uncommon. Most are late Victorian.*

Below: *Bermondsey Street, London. From 1874 to 1886, the Society for Photographing the Relics of Old London recorded many such buildings faced with destruction.*

Above right: *An advertisement by Lancaster and Sons. The company manufactured large numbers of cameras and examples are fairly common.*

Above left: *A photograph of a little girl with a bottle, c. 1898. Using hand-held cameras, Paul Martin specialized in unposed photographs of ordinary people at work and play. He was one of the pioneers of what was to become known as 'photo-journalism'.*

Above left: *Among the novelties available towards the end of the century were photographic stamps. These were produced commercially and by amateurs using special copying cameras.*

Above right: *'Colossal Figure at Singa-Sarie, Java.' A woodburytype from a negative by W. Bently Woodbury. Although produced mechanically in coloured pigment, a woodburytype closely resembles an original photograph; a characteristic it shares with the carbon printing process with which it is often confused. The majority of carbon prints – usually by the Autotype Company – and woodbury types are to be found as book illustrations.*

Far left: *Edwardian portrait by Agnes Warburgh. The introduction of the cheap Brownie camera revolutionized popular photography and may, in part, be responsible for the relative lack of interest shown in the work of many photographers who were active in the early part of this century. Although it is beyond the scope of Victorian photography, it is perhaps an area which the collector, less interested in the historical aspect, might find rewarding.*

Above: *Cyclists belonging to the Queen's City of Edinburgh Rifle Volunteer Brigade riding along Princes Street, 1884. Photographer unknown.*

Left: *A cabinet photograph of the Moulin Rouge dancer, La Goulou, c. 1885. A number of French firms published photographs around the turn of the century purporting to show scenes from this famous cabaret and examples are not uncommon. Genuine portraits of known habituées are somewhat rare.*

Photographic Collections

There are a number of important photographic collections available to the public in Britain. In addition, most reference libraries and major museums possess old photographs that, although not on display, may be seen on request. Regional museums and historical societies are another useful source of information.

Frequently a collector may have early photographs that are of interest to a public or specialized collection. It is a pleasant gesture, if the owner is reluctant to part with the original, to allow a copy to be made for the collection's records. This can usually be done at no cost to the collector. The National Monuments Record and The National Portrait Gallery, both in London, are two bodies that welcome such offers from collectors. It is, however, always advisable to write to the Librarian or Keeper concerned before sending original photographs.

GREAT BRITAIN

The Barnes Museum of Cinematography,
St. Ives, Cornwall.
The Birmingham Museum of Science and Technology.
The Royal Scottish Museum, Edinburgh.
The Muniment Room, Guildford
(photographs by Lewis Carroll).
The Manchester Museum of Science and Technology.
The Sutcliffe Gallery, Whitby, Yorkshire.

LONDON

The Kodak Museum.
The Royal Photographic Society.
The Science Museum.
The Victoria & Albert Museum.
The National Portrait Gallery
(Photographic Collection) at 15, Carlton House Terrace.

Selected Reading List

Brown, Bryan.	*The England of Henry Taunt, Victorian Photographer.*	Routledge & Kegan Paul.
Castle, Peter.	*Collecting and Valuing Old Photographs.*	Garnstone Press
Cohen, Morton N.	*Lewis Carroll at Christchurch.*	National Portrait Gallery.
Coe, Brian.	*George Eastman and the Early Photographers.*	Priory Press.
Coe, Brian and Michael Millward.	*Victorian Townscape – The Work of Samuel Smith.*	Ward Lock
Ford, Colin.	*The Hill and Adamson Albums.*	Times Newspapers Ltd.
Gernsheim, Helmut & Alison.	*The History of Photography.*	Thames & Hudson.
Holmes, Edward.	*An Age of Cameras.*	Fountain Press.
Matthews, Oliver.	*Early Photographs and Early Photographers.*	Reedminster Publications.
Newhall, Beaumont.	*The History of Photography.*	Secker & Warburg.
Strong, Dr Roy and Colin Ford.	*An Early Victorian Album.*	Jonathan Cape.
Thomas, Dr. D. B.	*Cameras.*	H.M.S.O.
Thomas, Dr. D. B.	*The First Negatives.*	H.M.S.O.
Thomas, Dr. D. B.	*The Origins of the Motion Picture.*	H.M.S.O.
Thomas, Dr. D. B.	*The Science Museum Photograph Collection.*	H.M.S.O.